The Tenderness of God

The Tenderness of God

Daniel Bourguet

Foreword by Bob Ekblad

Translated from the French

 CASCADE *Books* · Eugene, Oregon

THE TENDERNESS OF GOD

Cascade Books
An Imprint of Wipf and Stock Publishers
199 W. 8th Ave., Suite 3
Eugene, OR 97401

www.wipfandstock.com

PAPERBACK ISBN: 978-1-4982-8179-9
HARDCOVER ISBN: 978-1-4982-8181-2
EBOOK ISBN: 978-1-4982-8180-5

Cataloguing-in-Publication data:

Names: Bourguet, Daniel.

Title: The Tenderness of God / Daniel Bourguet.

Description: Eugene, OR: Cascade Books, 2016.

Identifiers: ISBN 978-1-4982-8179-9 (paperback) | ISBN 978-1-4982-8181-2 (hardcover) | ISBN 978-1-4982-8180-5 (ebook)

Subjects: LSCH: God—Mercy | God (Christianity)—Love | Love—Religious aspects—Christianity | Bourguet, Daniel

Classification: BS1199.A53 B68 2016 (PRINT) | BS1199.A53 (EBOOK)

Manufactured in the U.S.A.   07/12/16

Contents

Translator's Note

FRENCH LANGUAGE HAS AN openness and delicacy of feeling about emotions, particularly as they relate to the physical, which has little counterpart in English, and is difficult to reproduce. The title of this book translates very simply as the "tenderness" of God, but thereafter there are two key phrases in the book that are difficult to adequately convey. The most difficult is "*la pudeur*" of God, which is a frequent ascription and crucial to the heart of the book. Dictionaries render it variously as modesty, delicacy, reserve; it has strong hints of shame and bashfulness of a maidenly nature. How can it be possible to relate this term to God? Well, it can in French, and the meaning is clearly one of great reserve about the open expression of a great love, tenderness on the part of One who is infinitely sensitive and liable to pain, a Person who is considerate of others, and of very great delicacy and fineness of feeling. How are we to express this in English? It has been managed in this translation by using different words at different times as seemed fit—reserve, care, delicacy, reticence, modesty, propriety, decency; the default position has been modesty. A second difficulty is with the phrase "*emeut aux entrailles*," literally "moved to the entrails," and English translators of the Bible have had trouble at this point with the Greek word *splangna*; the KJV use of "bowels" is not really very helpful today, nor is "entrails"! "Guts" has been used in places; "moved inwardly" or "in the inner parts," following the Psalmist in the KJV, "you have desired truth in the inward parts," has often seemed best. Each time words that endeavor to convey these ideas appear, the reader is invited to invoke the range of meaning; we need to understand the physical aspect of the French words.

Foreword

THE PUBLICATION OF DANIEL Bourguet's books in English is a valuable contribution to the literature of contemplative theology and spirituality that will nourish and inspire the faith of all who read them. Daniel Bourguet, a French Protestant pastor and theologian of the Huguenot tradition, lives as a monk in the mountainous Cévennes region in the South of France. There at his hermitage near Saint-Jean-du-Gard, Daniel maintains a daily rhythm of prayer, worship, Scripture reading, theological reflection, and spiritual accompaniment. All of his books flow out of a life steeped in love of God, Scripture, and the seekers who come to him for spiritual support.

I first met Daniel Bourguet in 1988 when my wife, Gracie, and I moved from rural Central America to study theology at the Institut Protestant de Théologie (IPT), where he taught Old Testament. The IPT is the Église protestante unie de France's[1] denominational graduate school in Montpellier, France.

Prior to our move to France while ministering among impoverished farmers in Honduras in the 1980s, we had come across the writings of Swiss theologian Wilhelm Vischer and French theologian Daniel Lys by way of footnotes in Jacques Ellul's inspiring books. Vischer had written a three-volume work entitled *The Witness of the Old Testament to Christ*, of which only volume 1 is translated into English.[2]

1. Then the Église réformée de France.
2. Wilhelm Vischer, *The Witness of the Old Testament to Christ*, vol. 1, *The*

That book, along with a number of articles and Daniel Lys' brilliant *The Meaning of the Old Testament*,[3] exposed us to a community of Bible scholars who articulated a continuity between the Old and New Testaments that was highly relevant then and now. This connection would ultimately lead me to Bourguet.

We experienced firsthand how a literal reading of the Old Testament in isolation from the New Testament confession that Jesus is both Lord and Christ (Messiah) brings great confusion, division, and even destruction. In rural Honduras churches often distinguish themselves by selective observance of Old Testament laws and use certain Old Testament stories to inspire fear of God as punishing judge. In North America Christians were drawing from the Old Testament to justify the death penalty and US military intervention in Central America and beyond.

Wilhelm Vischer himself had been an active resister of Nazism from his Old Testament teaching post inside Germany. He resisted the misuse of Scripture to justify anti-Semitism, nationalism, and war, insisting on the importance of the Old Testament for Christian faith at a time when it was being dismissed. He was consequently one of the first professors of theology to be pressured to leave his post and eventually depart Nazi Germany before World War II, and served as Karl Barth's pastor in Basel after he too left Germany. After the war, the church in France, having been widely engaged in resistance to Nazism and deeply encouraged by Barth, invited Vischer to be the professor of Old Testament at the IPT in Montpellier.

Ellul, Vischer, Lys and other French theologians were offering deep biblical reflection that led us to look into theological study in France.[4] We wrote the IPT about their graduate program and discov-

Pentateuch, trans. A. B. Crabtree (London: Lutterworth, 1949).

3. Daniel Lys, *The Meaning of the Old Testament* (Nashville: Abingdon, 1967).

4. We were able to study with pastor and New Testament professor Michel Bouttier, who was also trained by Vischer and published broadly, including a commentary on Ephesians and a number of collections of provocative articles. Elian Cuvillier followed Michel Bouttier and is currently Professor of New Testament at

ered that Vischer had long since retired after training several generations of pastors. His protégée, Daniel Lys, had recently retired but was
still available. In Lys' place was his doctoral student Daniel Bourguet,
who also had been trained by Vischer. The IPT welcomed us with a
generous scholarship and we were soon making plans to learn French
and move to Montpellier.

We were eager for help to understand Scripture after being immersed in Bible studies with impoverished farmers in war-torn Honduras. Disillusioned with America after being engaged in resisting US
policy in Central America, we felt drawn to reflect from a different
context. We reasoned that studying in a Protestant seminary with a
history of persecution in a majority Catholic context would prove valuable. We left Tierra Nueva in the hands of local Honduran leaders and
moved to Montpellier two months early to study French and began
classes in September 1988.

Daniel Bourguet taught us Hebrew and Old Testament in ways
that made the language and text come alive. He invited students into
his passion and curiosity as we pondered both familiar and difficult
passages of Scripture. I remember continually being surprised at how
seriously Daniel took every textual critical variant, even seemingly ir-
relevant ones. He masterfully invited and guided us to both scrutinize
and contemplate each variant in its original language until we understood the angle from which ancient interpreters had viewed the text.
Daniel modeled an honoring of distinct perspectives as we studied the
history of interpretation of each passage. He sought to hold diverse
perspectives together whenever possible, yet only embraced what the
text actually permitted, exemplifying fine-tuned discernment that inspired us.

Daniel's thorough approach meant he would only take us through
a chapter or two per semester. This meant we took entire courses on
Genesis 1-2:4, on Abraham's call in Genesis 12:1-4, and on Jeremiah
31, Exodus 1-2, Psalms 1-2 and others. In each of his courses he

the IPT, writing many high quality books and articles.

included relevant rabbinic exegesis, New Testament use of the Old Testament, and the church fathers' interpretations. Daniel imparted his confidence that God speaks good news now as he accompanied us in our reading, making our hearts burn like those of the disciples on the road to Emmaus—and inspiring us to want to do this with others. In alignment with Vischer and Lys he demonstrated through detailed exegesis of Old Testament texts how God's most total revelation in Jesus both fulfills and explains these Scriptures, making them come alive through the Holy Spirit in our lives and diverse contexts.

While living in France every summer Gracie and I traveled from France to Honduras, spending several weeks sharing our learning with Tierra Nueva's Honduran leadership and leading Bible studies in rural villages before returning back for classes in the Fall. We had pursued studies in France with the vision of bringing the best scholarship to the service of the least in a deliberate effort to bridge the divide between the academy and the poor. Our experience of the rare blend of scholarship and pastoral sensitivity, which you will see for yourself in his books, contributed to us feeling called back to the church, into ordained ministry and back to the United States to teach and minister there. I benefited from his being my dissertation supervisor as I continued to integrate regular study into our ministry of accompanying immigrants and inmates as we launched Tierra Nueva in Washington State.

Daniel Bourguet's writings are like high-quality wine extracted from vineyards planted in challenged soil. Born in 1946 in Aumessas, a small village in the Cévennes region of France, Daniel Bourguet grew up in the heartland of Huguenot Protestantism, which issued from the Reformation in the sixteenth century. He pursued studies of theology at the IPT in Montpellier, including study in Germany, Switzerland and at the Ecole Biblique in Jerusalem. In lieu of military service, Daniel served as a teacher in Madagascar. He was ordained as a pastor in the Église réformée de France in 1972, serving parishes from 1973 to 1987. Daniel wrote his doctoral dissertation[5] while serving as

5. See Daniel Bourguet, *Des métaphores de Jérémie*, Paris : J. Gabalda, 1987.

a full-time parish pastor—a common practice in minority Protestant France, where teaching positions are scarce and pastors are in high demand. This practice often proves fruitful for ordinary Christians and theologians alike, deepening reflection and anchoring theologians in the church and world.

During our residential studies in Montpellier from 1988 to 1991, Gracie and I witnessed Daniel's interest in the early monastics and fathers of the Eastern church. In 1991 Daniel became prior of La Fraternité Spirituelle des Veilleurs (Spiritual Fraternity of the Watchpersons) and felt called to be a full-time monk, leaving the IPT in 1995 for a year in a Cistercian monastery in Lyon before moving to his current site in Les Cévennes in 1996.

Joy, simplicity, and mercy are the three pillars of Les Veilleurs, an association of laypeople and pastors founded by French Reformed pastor Wilfred Monod in 1923 (with a Francophone membership of four hundred in 2013). Members of this fellowship commit to pursuing daily rhythms of prayer and Scripture reading, including noontime recitation of the Beatitudes, Friday meditation on the cross, regular engagement with a faith community on Sundays, and spiritual retreats and reading that benefits from universal devotional and monastic practices. Les Veilleurs has served to nourish renewal in France and influenced the founding of communities such as Taizé. Under Daniel Bourguet's leadership Les Veilleurs thrived. As a member of Les Veilleurs I attended many of his annual retreats, witnessing and experiencing the vitality of this movement firsthand.

Daniel Bourguet's teaching and writing since his departure from his professorship at the IPT in 1995 have focused primarily on equipping ordinary Christians to grow spiritually through engaging in devotional practices such as prayer, Scripture reading and contemplation. Other works that will hopefully appear in English include reflections on asceticism, silence, daily prayer and the trinity. All but three of Daniel's twenty-five or so books are based on his spiritual retreats offered to pastors and retreatants with Les Veilleurs. He has offered retreats to

Roman Catholic, Orthodox, and Protestant communities throughout France and Francophone Europe and is widely read and appreciated as a theologian who bridges divergent worlds and nourishes faithful Christian practice in France. Daniel Bourguet made his first and only visit to the United States in 2005, offering a spiritual retreat in Washington State. He accompanied me to Honduras on that same trip just after Hurricane Katrina ravaged the country, teaching Tierra Nueva's leaders and accompanying me as I led Bible studies and ministered in rural communities.

Daniel left his role as prior in 2012 and now continues his daily offices, receives many seekers for personal retreats, and offers occasional retreats where he lives and writes. In alignment with the early monastic commitment to manual labor, Daniel weaves black and white wool tapestries of illustrations of Biblical stories done by pastor and painter Henri Lindegaard. Daniel's unique contribution includes his Trinitarian approach to biblical interpretation wherein he reads Scripture informed by the early church fathers, with special sensitivity to how texts bear witness directly but also indirectly to Jesus, the Father and the Holy Spirit.

Daniel Bourguet models an approach to Scripture and spirituality desperately needed in our times. He reads the Bible with great confidence in God's goodness, discovering through careful reading, prayer, and contemplation insights that feed faith and inspire practice. Daniel's deliberate reading in communion with the church fathers brings the wisdom of the ages to nourish the body of Christ today. His tender love for people who come to him for spiritual support, and the larger church and world inform every page of his writing, inspiring like practice. May you find in this book refreshment, strength, and inspiration for your journey as you are drawn into deeper encounters with God.

Bob Ekblad

Mount Vernon, WA
July 7, 2016

Preface

THIS BOOK REPRISES TEACHING given in the form of a retreat of the Fraternité Sprituelle des Veilleurs in different places in the course of 2009. In retreats, as with preaching, bibliographic references are left to one side; they might have had a place in marginal notes, but I have preferred to keep them to a minimum in order to stay close to the style of a retreat, as if the reader had also been invited to take part in a retreat through this book.

The people present at these retreats were believers, Christians, and the reader will see that my remarks assume this. Nothing has been changed here, so a reader who is not a believer will undoubtedly feel uncomfortable at times; for the host of questions that will arise for such a reader I ask pardon; however, to go on a retreat is to retire from the world for a time to be face to face with God and the teaching at a retreat is a means to that encounter; for this, a person would have to be a believer. You need to know this before starting to read the book; I am speaking here as if at a retreat, to a reader who is a believer.

Finally, again as if on a retreat, I have kept the elements of an oral style. You are addressed here as a "reader friend," in the form of a dialogue, a dialogue that proposes to be no more than an overture to the most sublime of dialogues, that with God.

So there we are, my reader friend! May your dialogue with God find something here to nourish it.

Benediction

I honor you, Father
who have given me the immense grace
of your sweet and benevolent presence
during the time of preparation
and making of this little book,
despite the darkness of my mind
and the feebleness of my love for you.
You have also accorded me the grace
of introducing and leading me a little
into the mystery of your humble and modest tenderness.

When I have bowed before you
you have overwhelmed my heart
and immersed me in wonderment
as you welcome my worship with love
in the silence of your sweet and benevolent presence.

Father,
I bow before you afresh
to bring thanks once again,

and to ask you to bless each of your children
who now hold in their hand this little book.
May you give them the grace, wrapping them round
with your infinite tenderness,
to lead them in silence to read by your Holy Spirit,
to touch in the very depths of the soul
and open them always more
to the infinite mystery of your humble and modest tenderness.
May you grant each one
in your immense love
despite the imprecisions and clumsiness found in my words
that the gift of their love for you may grow much stronger
and that their heart may fill with eternal joy.
I pray in the name of your Well-Beloved Son Jesus Christ,
the Son of your tenderness.
Amen.

CHAPTER 1

Introduction

Invited to Write

THE TENDERNESS OF GOD . . . these simple words are so great, so far beyond understanding, so holy, that there is little to do but prostrate oneself on the ground in silence! Such a subject certainly cannot be approached as simply a theme for reflection to satisfy our intellectual curiosity; it is a mystery, an unfathomable mystery, which plunges us into the depths of the heart of God.

The tenderness of God; the subject is enough to cause one's lips to be sealed forever in humble silence.

I would never have dared to speak of such a great mystery had I not been invited to do so by my spiritual father, Father Etienne, who one day said to me simply, "You know, Daniel, it would be good if you spoke to us about the tenderness of God." I accepted this word in profound silence and I prayed . . .

It took me many years of preparation to be able write what follows, but I have to own, reader friend, that I am very glad I took on this task; I have received so much in the process. Also, I believe it is very important for our modern world to lift its eyes towards the mystery of the humble and modest tenderness of God. There is not very much material which speaks in this way.

The Thirst for Tenderness

Another factor that impels me to write is the thirst for tenderness among the people around us; there are so many, young and old, who are ready to undertake almost anything, do anything, no matter what, because of this longing; and for so many of them, young and old, it becomes a hopeless search; they never suspect, far less know, that the most extraordinary tenderness is God's, that the very source of all tenderness is in him. When I think about this yearning and of the many ways people can go wrong, I realize for myself how marvelous it is to be able to go to the source and draw directly from him; to be able to drink in silence from God himself and, as I prepared to write, to seek from him the words that would convey the great, hidden beauty of his tenderness.

Lord my God, I know myself quite unworthy to enter even a little into the mystery of yourself; have pity on me and help me! Lead me by your Holy Spirit! Keep me from obscuring your secrets when I need to express the inexpressible!

The Father through the Son and in the Holy Spirit

Before approaching and examining some biblical texts in which the tenderness of God is to some extent unveiled, it seems a good idea to prepare ourselves with some introductory remarks that may help, I hope, to open us up a little, with the help of the Holy Spirit.

Christ is the very incarnation of the tenderness of God; he, in absolutely first place, reveals it to us, and it is surely with him that we must begin. He reveals it to us in his teaching, in his actions, his attitudes, in his manner of life. His being itself is steeped in the tenderness of the Father, with a great sense of modest reserve[1] which wonderfully reflects the reserve of his Father; this is something we should be able readily to understand because tenderness and reserve are just as inseparable in us. Jesus comes, then, to transmit with an overflow of humility the tenderness of his Father; the main difficulty for me is to arrive at a proper respect for this and treat it with appropriate care. You can see the extent to which I feel the obstacles to elaborating the subject; I can only ask the Lord to help me not to spoil anything or do anything that might in any way tarnish what is beyond understanding.

Lord Jesus Christ, Son of God, have mercy on me!

Christ's tenderness becoming incarnate means it is certainly more accessible to us than that of his Father; it became flesh of our flesh. It opens us up and leads us to that of the Father, so we might have begun by speaking of the tenderness of the Son, but, unfortunately, there are constraints of time. It would take too long to examine the tenderness of the Son first and then proceed further to that of the Father; since there isn't the time to properly investigate both themes, I have chosen to prioritize the tenderness of the Father, and will speak of the Son only in so far as this reveals the Father. It is on the latter, then, that we will dwell at leisure, taking time to reflect deeply, through the Son and in the Holy Spirit, without whom it is impossible to contemplate the mystery of the Father. As I say this, reader friend, you will appreciate that, in the end, pondering the tenderness of the Father, through the Son and in the Holy Spirit, leads us into the mystery of the Holy Trinity. This further explains how much one feels a pull towards the silence of wonderment.

Holy Trinity have mercy on me!

---

1. *Pudeur*; see Translator's Note.

Help from the Church Fathers _____

The church fathers have helped me greatly in the preparation of the book, in a somewhat paradoxical way. They themselves say hardly anything about the tenderness of God, not because the subject was unknown to them, but more because of their true sense of godly reserve, which, I think, greatly exceeds mine; they knew the wisdom of silence, of worshipful contemplation of such a profound mystery. From the few phrases I have been able to glean from reading the fathers, I understood that they had in fact profoundly contemplated the mystery of the tenderness of God, and that they had respected it by adopting a careful silence. They had tasted the humble and marvelous tenderness of God and were deeply affected by it.

A most beautiful example of the extreme reserve of the fathers[2] with regard to the tenderness of God is that of Calliste and Ignace Xanthopouloi who, in the fourteenth century, wrote a "spiritual century." Right at the outset of this lengthy treatise of a hundred pages they speak of God as "the Father who loves tenderly," using a term (*philostorgos*) to denote this tender love that is not found in the Bible, and can only have come from what they discovered of God in their own lives. Then, having so positioned their writing in the light of the tender love of God, they do not speak of it at all throughout the remainder of the work. What these two fathers experienced of the tenderness of God remains shrouded in the silence of delicacy.

This quasi silence of the fathers troubled me at times, to the point of causing me to think that I, in turn, would also do well to be quiet. However, what I have received from them in other ways has encouraged me to write, to share with you what only can be glimpsed in their writings; I feel that I am imparting their thoughts.

2. The author use the term loosely in this paragraph. (Trans.)

A Passage between Two Reefs _____

Another factor that encourages me to write on the tenderness of God is the observation of two failings that misrepresent it, two reefs to be avoided if we are to restore and preserve the beauty of its mystery.

The first failing is a sort of rose-water sentimentalism. Among some of our contemporaries there is a way of speaking of God and of his love that seems to me somewhat mawkish, marsh-mallowish; the tenderness of God has nothing of that.

Opposed to this is another failing, another reef just as dangerous, which lies in refusing to envisage God as having emotions. Some believers today have indeed deliberately opted not to give any place to the emotions of God, and, in so far as tenderness is also a form of emotion, they deny the fact of his tenderness.

These then are the two reefs between which we must push to find a way that does not compromise either the contemplation of mystery or the practice of a life in love relationship with God.

The Testimony of Abba Poemen _____

After these few remarks, it seems a good idea to propose to you now a text that has helped me not to fall into the errors just indicated, and a most beautiful example of what can be found in the fathers. It is a short text concerning one of the desert fathers, a fifth-century text from the monastic world of the Egyptian desert:

"Certain elders went to visit Abba Poemen and asked him, 'In your opinion, when we see brothers fall asleep while at divine office, is it needful to help them stay awake when they should be watching?' He told them, 'For myself, when I see a brother dozing, I lay his head on my knees and help him to rest'" (Apophthegm 666).

Here we have a text that reveals in Abba Poemen a man of great tenderness. What is related of him is certainly very touching, but you might say to me that we are dealing with an entirely human tenderness and that it does not directly concern the tenderness of God. This has some truth; but indirectly there is, all the same, something transmitted to us of God and his tenderness. What makes me say this is that the text records a meeting of "elders," that is to say, those responsible for small groups of monks. These elders, like Abba Poemen, are spiritual fathers, charged as such to bear witness to what they have perceived of the love of God the Father before the brothers who live alongside them. This meeting of elders addresses a question that unites all of them in their concern to be good witnesses to God's fatherly love. As such, Abba Poemen's response to the question of the other elders expresses more than just his human attitude, full of tenderness, but it also speaks of the attitude in which he, as a spiritual father, endeavors to communicate what he experienced of the tenderness of God.

Silent Tenderness

What does Abba Poemen help us to understand about God's tenderness? His gesture of tenderness towards the sleeping brother is accomplished without the slightest word, and, happily, without even waking him! I believe that in acting this way, Abba Poemen wished to testify to the tenderness of God, which may also surround us wordlessly, in total silence. Abba Poemen is blessed in helping us discover something essential about God's silence; that it may be full of the humble and delicate tenderness of God towards us. How wonderful to know this when we so easily perceive the silence of God as negative! This should help us to be attentive in our life, as in our reading of the Bible, to the fact that there are silences of God that are replete with extreme tenderness.

It is also worth noting in the text about Abba Poemen that the word "tenderness" is not used. The word is absent, but the tenderness is present. The same goes for God in the Bible; the word "tenderness" is rarely applied to God, while his tenderness nevertheless is always present, behind the words, between the words, at times even in the silences of the text! All this shows the way we need to redouble our attention if we are to perceive in the Scriptures, as well as in our lives, something that is present very discreetly.

Tenderness Unknown to Its Beneficiary

As a final comment on the patristic text, I would like to stress that the principal interested party, the beneficiary of the tenderness of Abba Poemen, is fast asleep, and has no awareness of the tenderness that embraces him. This is also most instructive for us: we don't appreciate correctly, and sometimes not at all, the divine tenderness that surrounds us. We are surely, spiritually, so deeply asleep. . . . Unknown to us, the Lord silently lays our head upon his knees and watches over us with tenderness, with that infinite tenderness of which he is so profoundly possessed.

We also discover here the extreme delicacy with which the tenderness is accompanied. If the brother were not asleep, Abba Poemen would beyond doubt not have presumed to act as he did, contrary as it would have been to propriety. But since the brother was asleep, the father could permit himself to put off a little the veil of reserve and allow his tenderness to show. God does the same for us; when we sleep, his tenderness is manifest, but when we awake from our slumber he keeps himself discreetly veiled in modesty.

If the tenderness of Abba Poemen escaped the sleeping brother, without doubt it did not escape the other brothers present at divine office. They were witnesses without being beneficiaries, but also without being altogether excluded; they knew their Abba well enough to know that he was full of the same tenderness towards them, though they would not experience it directly either. Something similar applies to our Bible reading; while reading, we see in the tenderness of God towards others that which he has for us. We may indeed never have felt the tenderness that God entertains towards us, but we need to submit to the evidence that this tenderness concerns us as well as others; we are also his children. God's modesty is such that it hides from us the tenderness by which we are secretly surrounded. Be careful not to think that the tenderness of God is for others and not for ourselves, merely on the slender grounds that we don't feel it.

Love's Palette

"God is love"; here is a fundamental affirmation that we find in the Bible (1 John 4:8, 16). It is fundamental, yet at the same time so little used by the biblical writers, so shrouded in reserve, that it is only found in this one place. Something that is rarely spoken is not necessarily secondary, and might well be of first importance; this is particularly true where a person's modesty is engaged.

"God is love." We find these words only from the pen of John, who rested his head on Jesus' breast (John 13:23). He experienced the mystery of the divine tenderness in such a profound way that he alone was able to get to the heart of words and say what nobody before him had managed to say.

"God is love." This expression is the synthesis of John's spiritual walk, and also the synthesis of the faith of Israel and the whole church. The whole Bible is saturated with this reality, though, except for this passage of John, in a diffuse way, just as I believe the whole Bible is permeated with the tenderness of God, though so rarely expressed.

If I blend here love and tenderness it is because tenderness cannot be considered apart from love; it is a facet of love, one of the colors on love's palette. I would also say that it is without doubt the most delicate color, the most subtle, the finest flower of love. Tenderness is so delicate and fine that it can easily pass unperceived, and borders on the inexpressible. It is often necessary to push in between words to find it; it is at times necessary to attend only to the intonation of words to perceive it; as you know, it can often appear in a simple look or in a silence.

Just as colors can be deployed in a range from the loudest and most garish to the most tender, the love of God is described in the Bible in the strongest words and silences and also in the gentlest words and silences. It would take too long here to review all the facets of the love of God, so I would like to look at just the two extremes, making use of an image to do so.

From Anger to Tenderness

It is not going to come as a surprise, then, to hear that I believe the love of God can be violent. I believe that we are engaged with this violence particularly when the Bible speaks of God's anger. Human anger is most often devoid of any love, but with God, who is nothing but love, his anger is a facet of his love; it is one of the expressions of the violence of his love. More precisely, the anger of God is a manifestation of his wounded love. When love is wounded, there is a reaction and it is expressed with passion, and this is equally so with God; his anger gives expression to his wounded love. Once I had understood this, all the biblical texts on the anger of God became beautifully clear to me, and caused anything that could offend to disappear.

The picture I wish to use to describe divine love, which ranges from the violence of passion to tenderness, without ceasing to be love, is that of a wave. In the heart of the ocean, a wave can be so violent that it is capable of overturning a ship and causing it to sink. Then this wave, monumental though it is, as it makes its journey across the ocean, continually loses power as it approaches land, becoming a simple ripple on the shore. Then it is no longer capable of sinking a ship; on the contrary, it tickles the sole of the foot of a little child, not to scare, but causing delighted laughter with its gentle caress. The same wave that can destroy a ship in its violence can also caress a child with tenderness and fill the child with pleasure. In the same way divine love is able in its anger to extinguish powerful enemies in the depths of the ocean of evil; and can also contain and soften its violence as it draws close to us to spare us, to caress the wounded soul with endless tenderness, restoring it to well-being.

Engaging Wounded Souls

Knowing this about the different shades and intensity of the love of God, we might well ask ourselves whether it is opportune to spend time on what is most delicate in the love of God; it might be better spent pressing non-believers with the vigorous love of God, to lead them to believe; or proclaiming his love as a tonic to strengthen believers in their faith and in their engagements with the world. Might we not be wasting time dwelling upon subtle refinements of the tenderness of God? Surely the urgency of spiritual combat requires strong words, a tonic to season us for the fray, to help us fight with courage!

It is unquestionable that the violence of spiritual combat requires of us that we be tough, but it is exactly because the combat is violent that it leaves numbers of wounded by the wayside, wounded souls who need to be approached with softness and tenderness if they are to be cared for. You are bound to meet such wounded people, as I do. Indeed, I encounter them often; it is they who make me aware of the need for us to stop and spend time on the tenderness of God, to keep it always in mind as part of our attitude towards the hurting. There are so many wounded people today and it is particularly of these that I think in writing this book, to help them back onto their feet before they return to their commitments.

The church is made up of believers who fight with courage on the frontline; it also includes the lame, sidelined for more or less time before taking up arms again. For the one, the love of God should be a fortifying tonic, and for the others there should be a redoubling of tenderness. The same person can be in the battle one day and in hospital the next!

Among wounded souls today there are many who may be hurt by traumas of such a depth that the slightest word, the least word even of love, can hurt them. There are wounds to the soul that are, so to speak, untouchable because the least contact revives them. There have been times when simply hearing the word "love" as I speak of the love of God has caused a violent reaction, the word awakens so much suffering. The same thing happens with the word "God," which for some has become a source of pain; the same again with the word "father" or with other words that are essential in formulating the Christian message. What are we to say then? What words do we use to engage a wounded soul without reawakening the suffering? Well, at times there are words we can speak with the greatest tenderness possible, pleading with God at the same time to instill in our tenderness something of his, that his tenderness may warm the soul and reinvigorate it without opening the wound again; at times, indeed, there may be no more than the silence of listening or a look of tenderness to lay as a balm upon the wound. I do believe that, through our tenderness, the tenderness of God can flow caressingly to touch the untouchable pain of a wounded soul.

If this is so, given the number of wounded souls who bestrew the world today, it is entirely opportune to spend time meditating on the tenderness of God. Perhaps you are one of these wounded, reader friend; perhaps many of those around you are such? Then you understand how important it is to pursue our reflections on this subject.

Christ to Lead Us

When we speak of tenderness, we are fully immersed in the realm of the emotions. In this realm we get down to real messy life, a stew of the best and the worst. There are negative emotions, suspicions, troubles, impurities, and perhaps it is for this reason that some people refuse to think of God as having emotions. Such a judgment is, however, excessive and decidedly risks throwing out the good with the bad; there are other emotions of real beauty, which definitely have their place in God. Tenderness is one of these; in God it is a perfectly pure emotion, noble, beautiful, and holy. Tenderness is a reality of human love and it is also a reality of divine love. As an emotion, I believe that we need to address the question of the tenderness of God.

The longer I dwell on God's tenderness the more I discover that we are dealing with a flower of incomparable beauty, a flower of such delicacy that one fears so much as to touch it. It is enough to contemplate it and to sense its incomparably subtle perfume. I believe that the tenderness of God, sensed like this, is a caress to the soul.

But how should we talk about such a flower? I believe we need to ensure we do this with real authority, speaking as people who know just what to say, and to do this we need to turn to the pre-eminent authority, to Christ. He, more than anyone, is able to lead us on the road of God's tenderness. He alone is perfectly able to reveal it to us. As I have said, I do not wish to focus on the unique tenderness of Christ, but I address myself all the same to him that he may help us discover the tenderness of his Father.

Lord Jesus Christ, Son of God, have mercy on us!

The Teaching of Christ

Well considered, Christ meets our need in two ways: above all, in his teaching, then by the fact that he incarnates tenderness and reveals it in the way he lived. We will spend some time on this two-fold provision of Christ.

In his teaching, Jesus never used the word "tenderness." Nevertheless, make no mistake, he does speak of it, but with great care to respect what is in itself so delicate. It requires all of the delicacy of Christ to both reveal the tenderness of his Father and not diminish it.

In order to speak of God's tenderness with care, Jesus found it helpful to use parables. The parable has the extraordinary quality of permitting great delicacy, in so far as it enables you to speak of God without naming him, of his tenderness without naming it. An inattentive reader may find in the parables stories that are very human, stories of fathers, vineyards, kings . . . without realizing that, through the characters, God is to be seen. The parable permits, in effect, a veil of reserve to be placed over the feelings or emotions of God, hiding them in human stories.

The Father of the Prodigal Son

The most beautiful parable concerning the tenderness of God is certainly that told about the prodigal son, which is found in Luke 15. This extraordinary parable shows us a father, but he is never actually said to represent God; however, the whole context of this passage of the Gospel enables the understanding that through the father, in a veiled way, it is indeed God himself who is to be discovered; even then, in this little morality play, this God of supreme tenderness plays a relatively modest role.

Bearing in mind that you know the parable, I will reproduce only the verse that I believe is the high point of tenderness, describing the moment when the father finds the son after years of separation. "When the son was still far off his father saw him and his heart was moved with compassion; running to him, he fell on his neck and embraced him" (v. 20).

The father Jesus introduces here is particularly sensitive. It is for this reason that he sets off at a run to meet his son. Certainly he is longing to see the son, but also, the more he runs, the more he increases the distance between himself and the rest of his household, between himself and the eventual witnesses, so that these may not see the greeting between himself and his son. Tenderness does not look for the interest of witnesses; it protects itself against them. What passes here between the father and his son, hidden from view, the embrace of love soberly described by Jesus, is full of great tenderness.

The Silence of Tenderness

Consider again Abba Poemen and his gesture of tenderness towards his brother; remember how the gesture was unaccompanied by words. There is something similar in the parable. The father embraces the son without the least word for the simple reason that there are no words to express what fills his heart. His tenderness is enveloped in silence and this silence speaks of a love that is too great to be spoken. The fullness of the tenderness of love is beyond words. Through this parable Jesus reveals to us that this fullness of tenderness is in the Father God each time he re-finds one of us, one of his children who return to him after being estranged. What marvelous tenderness there is in the silence of God!

Certainly the silence is soon broken, but it is the son, not the father, who breaks it. The father would perhaps wish to suspend the silence for eternity. In this silence, the tenderness is so welcoming as to hang on the slightest word the son may speak. It is such a long time since the father heard the voice of his son! The silence of the father welcomes the repentance of the son. What an extraordinary teaching Jesus gives about the welcome God reserves for our prayer of repentance. The silence of tenderness is a jewel case in which to lay the prayer of the one who returns.

Hidden Tears

There is one expression in this verse that we would do well to underscore since it signifies the extreme delicacy with which Jesus speaks of
the emotion of God. "He fell on his neck. . . ." This expression is very
rare in the Scriptures; it is not found elsewhere, other than three times
in the book of Genesis (33:4; 45:14; and 46:29) and nowhere else. Each
time, the action so described is one of the reunion between two members of the same family and each time it is accompanied by tears. The
one who falls on the neck of the recovered relative sheds tears, which
he endeavors to hide, burying his face on the other's shoulder. These
tears are of such tenderness that they must be hidden; those of God
are so beautiful that Jesus finds no words to express them. Recalling in
God's case the expression from Genesis, he tells us, without mentioning them, of the tears God sheds in tenderness when the estranged one
returns to him. An overwhelming welcome is reserved by God for the
prodigal child that each of us is. Jesus delicately declines to say how far
the emotion of God extends.

Jesus never in his teaching used the word "tenderness," but what
he only evokes here leads us on into the infinite depth of the mystery
of God.

To Be Moved with Compassion

In this same verse again, it is worth noting another meaning which
lies in the Greek and which reveals, not the extent, but the source of
the tenderness: "he was moved to the heart, the guts."[3] This is the first
reaction of the father when he sees his son in the distance. This feeling
is of such force as to cause him to run, to fall on the neck of his son
and embrace him.

3. See introductory translator's note. (Trans.)

What Jesus says in this expression is of the order of a revelation, a very important revelation: tenderness has its source in the inner parts.[4] This is so new that Jesus is obliged to give a Greek word a sense it had not carried before. Previously the Greek word meant, "to eat the entrails of a victim offered in sacrifice" (cf. 2 Macc 6:8). Jesus leaves to one side the classical meaning of the verb to give it the sense retained thereafter by the authors of the New Testament: "to be moved to the heart/guts/inward parts/bowels." We will return to the link between tenderness and the inward parts, but I stop to reflect for a moment how Jesus was led to invent, to give a new sense to a word, in order to tell and reveal the profound origin of the tenderness of God.

Tenderness Incarnated

In order to underline this point I return to another point previously left unresolved. I have said that Jesus reveals the tenderness of God in his teaching, through the parables in particular. I have also said, without developing the point, that equally he embodied the tenderness of God; it is on this second point that I would like to pause, illustrating by an example that shows how the tenderness of Christ radiates that of his Father.

Luke's Gospel is alone in recounting the brief meeting of Jesus at Nain with a widow, on the day when she was following the funeral bier of her only son. Jesus sees this poor widow in her grief. He stands before this distressed woman who no longer has a husband and has just lost her only son, on whom alone she could depend. Who could henceforth comfort this widow and support her? Jesus knew the answer: there is no one but God, he whom the Scriptures call the "defender of widows" (Ps 68:6). Then, Luke tells us, Jesus was "moved

---

4. Another possible translation would recall the words of Jesus, "*out of his belly shall flow rivers of living water*" (John 7:38, KJV); the Greek is *koilia*, meaning a cavity, hollow, hence abdomen and also womb. (Trans.)

with compassion" (7:13); he was filled with strong emotion, by the very emotion of God, who from that time was the one who would care for this widow. Jesus, then, embodies the feelings of God, the defender of widows. He embodies them right to the heart of his being, from where the profound tenderness of God himself flows towards this widow.

Tenderness in the Tone of Voice

"Jesus was deeply moved"; in so describing the way Jesus felt, Luke makes us attentive to the tenderness of Jesus without going so far as to use the word "tenderness," no doubt out of delicacy, respecting the reserve of which his Master makes proof in the way he acts towards this woman. The rest of the account shows us indeed how Jesus demonstrated his tenderness to this widow, behaving with great delicacy. How then does he act? He does not, to be sure, fall on the neck of this woman as the father of the prodigal had on that of his son! Jesus did not make the slightest move that might offend propriety. He contents himself with addressing just one word to this widow: "Don't cry!" That is all, but it was enough; all the feeling of his heart, all his tenderness in one word. Of course, this simple statement need not be an expression of tenderness. Indeed, this "don't cry" could be spoken sharply, as a reproach, rebuking the person in tears. Everything, not just the word itself, but the intonation given it, is colored by the sentiment of the person speaking; anger, irritation, tenderness. . . . What lets us know what feeling informed Jesus is what Luke has just told us—"he was deeply moved"; in saying this Luke signifies that the words spoken to the widow were full of tenderness.

Tenderness is so delicate that it expresses itself not with a word but in the intonation given the word. How blessed Luke is in being able to hear in no more than the intonation of a word the tenderness that filled Jesus.

But what kind of tenderness exactly are we dealing with? Could it be a purely human tenderness? Why have I said earlier that the tenderness of Jesus is that of God?

An All-Powerful Gentleness

In responding to this story, comments might easily become trite and sentimental; this would betray the tenderness that Jesus shows. What in fact happens in the story? Immediately after the words addressed to the widow, Luke tells us that Jesus "touched the funeral bier," again a gesture of tenderness. It is the same sort of touch that you will have seen at a funeral when someone touches the coffin of the deceased. This gesture, never forceful, is always made with tenderness, like a caress. Now see how Jesus, after this tender gesture, begins to speak to the dead man so that he is revived: "Young man, I say to you, arise!" Then he returns the son to his mother, which again is an act of tenderness to comfort the widow.

What strikes me in all this is the extreme tenderness of Jesus, which contains in itself a power so great as to be capable of lifting the dead man off the bier and return him to life. There is definitely nothing sentimental here! It is a paradoxical tenderness in which extreme gentleness and extreme power are intimately mingled. This paradoxical tenderness could come from nowhere if not from God, as the crowd recognize in wonderment, saying, "God has visited his people" (v. 16). The crowd was blessed in being able to discern that God in his tenderness was revealing himself in the tenderness of Christ. Luke is also wonderfully blessed to be able to express the inexpressible, the all-powerful and all-gentle nature of the divine tenderness embodied in Christ. And it is true, as we shall see again in other biblical passages; the tenderness of God consists of a very great gentleness with which is blended astonishing power.

A Heart of Pity and Compassion _____

Turn back now to the Parable of the Prodigal Son. In speaking of the innermost feelings of the father, Jesus is indirectly speaking in some sort of the innermost parts of God the Father! We will have to spend some time on this point.

To hold only to the immediate sense of the word translated "innermost parts" would be to become trivial. Actually it borders on blasphemy. Jesus really doesn't give this parable to encourage an anatomical investigation of God! I won't go on since I am sure you know full well we're speaking of something quite different. By speaking of the innermost physical parts Jesus simply wishes to locate us in the area of emotions and feelings, on the palette of love's various colors. It is here that we must locate ourselves if we are to consider the spiritual depth of what Jesus tells us about the tenderness of God and of its source, which he says is deeply inward. It has to be so; anyone who has been moved by tenderness has felt at how a deep a level this feeling is born.

In the New Testament the word for "inward parts" is often linked to other words which can help us understand to what tenderness is directly related.

In Luke 1:78, the word is accompanied by the word "mercy" (in Greek *splagchna eleous*, literally, guts, bowels of mercy). The phrase is found here in the song of Zechariah, which celebrates God in the profundity of his mercy. We learn from this that the "inward parts" are also the source from which comes mercy.

In Colossians 3:12, the apostle Paul links our word to "compassion" (in Greek *splangchna oiktirmou*, literally, guts or bowels of compassion). And so here we learn that the inward parts are equally the source from which comes compassion.

Besides these two expressions where "inward parts" is associated with another word, there is one text where the word stands alone, in a pure state so to speak. In this case the word signifies quite simply "tenderness," which clearly shows that behind mercy and behind compassion we find tenderness. Each of these Greek turns of phrase shows that in the end tenderness rises from deep within and it can manifest itself in mercy or in compassion; according to the circumstances it can become merciful or compassionate. In just this way, compassionate tenderness is clearly seen in the attitude of Jesus towards the widow at Nain. It's a movement from deep inside that fills him with compassion for this woman. On the other hand, the deep inner feeling of the father of the prodigal son fills him with such mercifulness that his son can feel it directly and receive the pardon for which he longs.

Inward Parts and Tenderness

The New Testament text where the word *splagchnon* appears without any complement and has the sole sense of tenderness, is particularly beautiful, and reveals the apostle Paul in a guise we might not otherwise suspect of him, a man of astonishing tenderness. Here is what he writes to his brothers in Philippi: "I cherish you with the tenderness (*splagchnois*) of Jesus Christ" (1:8). I have to say that this verse turned the image I had of the apostle completely upside down.

Tenderness in a pure state, the tenderness that manifests as mercy or compassion; this is what the New Testament leads us to discover and opens before us as twin pathways along which I propose we travel. I have made some steps along these two pathways as I result of my experience. I wouldn't wish to prevent you from engaging with other expressions of tenderness, but my experience is, above all, of the Lord leading me in these two paths of tender mercy and tender compassion.

Tenderness as a Response to Suffering _____

We can say that in these two ways, God, in his tenderness, faces up to human suffering and responds to it, whether in mercy when confronted by suffering due to guilt, or in compassion towards suffering that is innocent.

Before going any further, I realize that what I am referring to as two pathways may at times form just one because, in God's sight, a person's suffering might be both culpable and innocent; the infinite tenderness of God may at the same time be both merciful and compassionate.

As you can see, our meditation on the tenderness of God is far from an unnecessary refinement; it helps us to discover how far God goes in giving the best of himself when faced with human suffering, whether innocent or guilty, and how this can help us to give the best of ourselves when faced with the suffering of others.

Tenderness and Mercy _____

It becomes immediately obvious that mercy needs to be closely tied to tenderness when we think simply on the level of human relations. You will certainly have experienced, at least once, a situation in which you have been led to either ask pardon of or extend pardon to someone. Undoubtedly you will have noticed the possibility that the pardon granted might even have a bad effect on the person who receives it. It could in fact be a mercy that hurts the other simply because it lacks tenderness, or perhaps because tenderness has been replaced by condescension or even contempt, "pity" in the worst sense of the word. Such mercy does not come from inward conviction but from a hard heart; it really does not deserve the name mercy. By contrast, forgiveness stemming from a real inner mercifulness does enormous good; it soothes, comforts, and consoles the one who has asked pardon. This type of mercy is full of tenderness and it is the tenderness that imparts any goodness to the beneficiary. This is the true connection between tenderness and mercy.

Looked at closely, we see again that it is in the *tone of voice* that the difference becomes apparent between mercy with tenderness and mercy without tenderness.

In God there is no mercy without tenderness. Tenderness and mercy gush out together from his inmost being; that's why his mercy never does harm. To the sinner who repents God comes with arms open wide, like the father of the prodigal, in his tender mercy. It is essential to know this truth if we are to experience it. Each time in your life that you are led to repentance towards God, be assured that in his Fatherly love he is most deeply moved and that his mercy is full of tenderness, even if the veil of his modesty does not permit you to feel his emotion. In the same way, without your feeling it and unknown to you, the Lord does give you his pardon and wraps you round with an infinite tenderness, which you can receive and welcome by faith.

Tenderness and Compassion

The connection between tenderness and compassion is also imperfect when it comes to human relations, but perfect with God.

You will certainly have experienced some kind of grief, for example, which will have meant receiving letters of condolence, and you will have noticed how some such letters, though full of compassionate words, contained nothing that really touched you, but that others, with just the same compassionate words really did touch you and brought consolation in your pain. The difference between the two compassions lies once again in the presence of tenderness in the tone of the words. If compassion consoles it is because it is full of tenderness. By contrast, when it fails to console it is because it lacks tenderness, because it is tenderness that touches the suffering heart and comforts.

Here again, in God, there is no compassion without tenderness. If in your innocent suffering you turn towards him, God always responds with tenderness, even if you do not feel it because it is veiled in his modesty, or for other reasons of which we will speak later.

The Strength of Tenderness

It seems a good idea at this point to investigate a little further the link between tenderness and compassion and that between tenderness and mercy. We need to see the way tenderness, as the source, has nothing weak about it, but on the contrary, as we saw above in the account of the widow of Nain, is an amazing power.

Compassion must be strong if it is to carry others in their suffering. We experience this realizing how tired we can be after engaging with someone we try to support in their trouble. Compassion needs to have great strength and this strength is received from tenderness; compassion without tenderness is unable to support others. Others know that they are not really being supported by a compassion which has no tenderness. This much is plain: tenderness gives compassion the power it needs. In itself, tenderness is amazingly strong, and so much more when God breathes his own tenderness into ours.

Mercy also needs to be strong if it is to pardon others their offences and free them from their weight of guilt. Where can this strength come from if not from tenderness? Anyone who receives from a forgiver a pardon without tenderness is well aware that the pardon is of no real value, as if the pardon was just casual, throw-away, with no real strength of conviction; he does not feel forgiven, freed from the weight of his fault. In contrast, the person who receives a pardon freighted with tenderness knows himself to have been really forgiven and realizes how the forgiveness has had the power to remove his fault. This much again is clear: tenderness is the very strength of mercy, thanks again to God who breathes the strength of his tenderness into human tenderness.

How wonderful tenderness is, made up entirely of gentleness, but a gentleness which is wonderfully strong!

What can be said of human tenderness can be taken to the extreme with God, who entirely alone, by his tenderness, can bear all the sufferings and even the sin of the entire world. How blessed was John the Baptist to see that the sin of the world was borne by a lamb (John 1:29), the paradoxical image of weakness and strength. What an amazing power of tenderness lives in the Son of the Father!

"I Am a God of Tenderness"

To say that God is merciful and compassionate comes back simply to saying that he is a God of tender mercy and tender compassion, and it says this without even pronouncing the word "tenderness." Here we find again the modest reserve of God, as well as of those who report it. Don't let this reserve cause you to doubt the tenderness, so present and hidden at the same time. I believe that here we are really touching into the mystery of God, the mystery of his tenderness. Reserve both veils and at the same time reveals a tenderness so profound that we lack words to express it.

Tenderness at one and the same time both hidden and revealed by God himself, this is the mystery to draw a little closer to now, not in curiosity but contemplatively and in adoration.

If people in the Bible celebrate God as a God of tenderness it is because one day God presented himself in this way, saying on that occasion something he has never repeated; not because he has changed his mind, surely, but simply because in his modesty he wants at the same time to both reveal his tenderness and to hide it.

The occasion to which I refer is reported in the book of Exodus, in chapter 34. The revelation of God on Mount Sinai is not some kind of solemn discourse, but rather a personal confidence; we see that Moses was the only person present to hear what was said, so in a way he was God's confidant, God counting him as his friend (Exod 33:11). On this day God appeared to him, not in a grand way, but very humbly, in a cloud, so that the cloud veiled the intimacy.

On this day, then, God said to his friend something he has never since repeated, "I am a God of tenderness" (Exod 34:6). French and English translations alike are marked by centuries of Christian tradition which has joined hands with the ancient Greek and Latin translations; this is why some, following the Latin (*deus misericors*), have translated this as "merciful God," while others, following the Greek (*théos oïktirmôn*), as "a God of compassion." Happily the Jerusalem Bible has perfectly respected the sense of the Hebrew word and translated "a God of tenderness."

The God of the Womb

This last translation seems the best to me because the adjective used in the Hebrew (*rakhum*) derives directly from the word *rekhem*, which denotes the womb; this has caused Chouraqui[5] to feel free to translate this with some finesse as *matriciel*, "of the womb."

With still more precision than the word for the inner parts,[6] the womb is, among the organs of the abdomen, the real seat of tenderness. Tenderness comes from the maternal organ, the source of life; it is drawn from this very feminine place, which gives life; it is so profoundly tied to life that God, himself the real giver of life, cannot be other than a God of tenderness, a God of the womb, a God with a womb, indeed a profoundly maternal God, to such a degree that we can speak of him as a maternal Father. We maintain as primordial for God the

---

5. An interesting recent French translation (Trans.)
6. Fr. *entrailles* (Trans.)

title of Father, faithful to the Bible, which never calls him Mother, but holding to the spirit that says this Father is profoundly maternal.

The church fathers perfectly understood this paternity/ maternity of God; for this reason they endeavored, in developing as spiritual fathers, to be spiritual mothers. We have seen this in the beautiful example of Abba Poemen, who, in taking onto his knees the head of the sleeping brother, behaves as a true maternal father. Elsewhere, when Seraphim of Sarov, another spiritual father, wrote to the monk Antoine, who had become the superior of a monastery, he counseled him, "Be a mother to the monks as much as a father. A loving mother supports the infirmities of the infirm with love; she cleans those who are soiled, washes them gently, peaceably, dresses them, warms, feeds, and consoles them. . . ."

A Man of the Womb

The feelings of the maternal organs are tied to the gift of life and awaken any time that the life given is endangered or in pain. A mother is deeply moved whenever she sees her child suffer.

We find this in the celebrated account, so full of fine feeling, of Solomon's judgment of the two women claiming the same child; it tells us that the king knew the true mother at the moment when "her womb yearned upon her son," when she heard the boy was to be cut in two (1 Kgs 3:26).

Given the way the Bible reveals the origin of tenderness in the womb, it is good, once again, not to react as if we were dealing with a strictly anatomical statement! Effectively, if a mother can feel this emotion in her womb, the Bible tells us that a man can also feel the same emotion, and so he also, in a way, has a womb!

So this expression, used in the account of the judgment of Solomon to describe the mother's emotion, is also found in Genesis to describe the feelings of a man, the patriarch Joseph, when he is re-united with his young brother Benjamin after years of separation. Joseph, the text tells us, "yearned upon his brother in his bowels/womb" (43:30). Joseph's feelings are so strong that he has to seek the refuge of a room apart to hide his tears.

An interesting aspect of this text is to note that Joseph and Benjamin were born of the same mother, Rachel, and that this mother had died in childbirth, at the birth of Benjamin. Benjamin had never known his mother, never benefited from her tenderness, and here he is receiving this tenderness from his older brother who feels for him a maternal tenderness. Strangely, Joseph behaves as a maternal father for his young brother.

It is good to know all this if we are to understand that Jesus undertook the office of maternal father each time that he is described as moved in the innermost parts. In this, Jesus is also the real incarnation of his motherly Father who he reveals to us in the Parable of the Prodigal Son. It is a wonderful parable, in which, curiously, the mother is absent, non-existent even, so the father is both father and mother.

Reader friend, if you have looked closely at Rembrandt's celebrated painting of the return of the prodigal son you will doubtless have noticed how the painter has given the father one masculine hand and one feminine, showing us that Rembrandt was aware of this motherly Father who Christ reveals.

More on Other Paths of Tenderness _____

The tenderness of God, the tenderness of a motherly Father, awakened by the suffering of his children, whether the suffering is blameworthy or innocent, this is what will particularly engage our attention in the following chapters. I am well aware, while limiting myself in this way, that I can barely skim the surface of the subject because the tenderness of God is so vast. Forgive me, reader friend, if I have hardly begun to uncover the depth, the length, the height of this tenderness, but I do know that the tenderness of God towards his children is always alive, whether they suffer or not; a mother does not wait until her child is suffering to show tenderness.

There is one particular text among others that will feed our meditation on this aspect of the tenderness of God. At the moment of Jesus' baptism, a time that does not involve suffering, when he is just going down into the water, his attitude provokes in God such emotion that he "parts" the heavens, as Mark puts it (1:10). He parts the heavens as a man full of emotion may rip his clothing (cf. Judg 11:35). Then we hear from the opened heaven these words full of tenderness, "You are my beloved Son, on whom I have set all my affection." Why this sudden outpouring of tenderness on the part of God the Father? Not because Jesus is in any pain, but rather, it seems to me, because of his humble self-abasement in the midst of the people, asking baptism humbly of the Baptist. The humble love of the Son, who offers himself to others, this too awakens the tenderness of God.

I am well aware that we could also speak of the romantic loving tenderness of God, so wonderfully evoked, as in a parable, in the Song of Songs. This is also a tenderness to be found in God and likewise does not wait for the suffering of its well-beloved to be manifest. This is also so true! But there we are, this is a vast and inexpressible subject. So, reader friend, please embrace the little that I am able to share about the tenderness of God faced with suffering, and for the rest, forgive me.

CHAPTER 2

Compassionate Tenderness

(Ezekiel 16:1–6)

F ROM THE VERY LONG sixteenth chapter of Ezekiel we will read no more than the first six verses, but I encourage you strongly to take the time to read the whole text because I am presupposing that you know it.

> *1. The word of the Lord came to me in these words. 2. Son of Man, make Jerusalem know her abominations! 3. You shall say, "Thus says the Lord to Jerusalem: by your origins and your birth you belong to the land of Canaan. Your father was an Amorite and your mother a Hittite. 4. At your birth, on the day when you were born, your cord was not tied; you were not washed in water to be cleansed; you were not rubbed with salt; you were not wrapped in cloth. 5. Nobody looked at you with pity to do one of these things with compassion. Instead you were cast out into the field, out of disgust for your soul, in that day when you were born. 6. But I passed by close to you; I saw you, struggling in your blood, and I said to you, while you were in your blood, "Live"; yes, I said to you while you were in your blood, "Live."*

A Precise Translation

In these first verses of the chapter we discover what happened on the day of the birth of little Jerusalem. The rest of the chapter tells us how the child grew, but we will dwell upon just the day of her birth.

With these verses I will begin by making a comment about the translation of verse 6 so that you won't be disturbed if the verse is translated differently in the Bible you use.

At the end of the verse some translators say this, "I said to you, 'Live in your blood'"; others translate, "I said to you, while you were in your blood, 'Live.'" The difference in the two ways of translating is to change the number of words spoken by God to the infant: for some it is "Live in your blood!" for others, simply, "Live!"

The two different ways of translating follow two ways of understanding nuances in the accentuation of Hebrew words. I have no wish for now to throw myself into a debate on this delicate point, which will not mean much to you if you don't know Hebrew. I will instead just give you my preference, which is that held to by quite a few translators, and consists in understanding here just the one word, "Live," as being what God said to the infant.

To Whom the Oracle Was Spoken _____

This oracle is intended for Jerusalem, that is to say, not a person but a collective group, described in image form as a person. This is a most important fact to underscore because it profoundly affects the way we read the text.

The fact that we have here an image in no way lessens the truth contained in the text; the truth is simply veiled in the image, which leaves us once again aware of the importance of the delicacy which throws a veil over truth. This is similar to the parables, where the truth of God is veiled behind the human personalities in the story. Here, the truth of God's life with the people of Jerusalem is veiled by the image of the little girl. Each inhabitant of Jerusalem can feel him or herself concerned here—even the men and the old, everyone—though none of them is described as actually present at the birth of the city. Here we have the image acting as a veil, making us sensitive and careful about all we discover of God's tenderness. Each inhabitant of Jerusalem can feel him or herself to be involved in this tenderness, without being so directly.

At issue here is Jerusalem and also, as we shall see, the tenderness of God for this city; but before proceeding further, to investigate this possible tenderness, we must also see if the text concerns us, you and me.

In one sense if, like me, you were not born in Jerusalem, you may not feel yourself to be an interested party in the text, and read it simply as a witness of what happened to someone else. But I would like to suggest another reading, one that will lead us to feel centrally involved in the text. How can this be? Jerusalem is the city where the temple is found, that is to say, the place where God meets with humanity. Today, according to the Bible, each of us has in himself or herself a place, difficult to delimit no doubt, but a place where God comes to meet us. This is why the apostle Paul can say, "we are the temple of God" (2 Cor 6:16). We are indeed the temple of God and we are this in a twofold way; together, collectively, we are the temple of God, and each one of us, individually, is also the temple of God. If you subscribe to this idea, then we are all involved in our text; being in ourselves the temple of God, *we* are Jerusalem. I am going to read this oracle, then, as being individually addressed to each of us, though your birth, like mine, was nothing like what is described here; the description is an image, but an image conveying profound truth.

When the prophet Ezekiel received the text, the temple in Jerusalem was in great danger (v. 39), threatened with destruction because of the base acts and immoralities of the city, immoralities worse than those of Sodom (v. 47). The difference, however, between Jerusalem and Sodom is that God was bonded in love to Jerusalem (v. 8), and that he swears fidelity to her despite everything (v. 60), so that if she retains life it is thanks to the indestructible and eternal loyalty of God in his love towards her. In this we can also see ourselves as implicated.

Suffering by Omission _____

Let us now return to the day of birth of the one with whom God was love-struck.

This chapter of Ezekiel is introduced with the use of the word "abomination" to denounce the misdeeds of Jerusalem, but make no mistake about this! The abominations committed by Jerusalem are those of her adulthood and not hers in her day of birth. On that day little Jerusalem[1] is presented to us by God himself as perfectly innocent. If that day there was any abominable behavior it was rather that of her parents. But we need to avoid any judgment because even God doesn't impose any on the parents of Jerusalem. His interest is only in the child, and if his interest is full of tenderness towards her, it is not the loving tenderness that he will evince for her later when little Jerusalem has become an adolescent (vv. 7–8); this is the tenderness of compassion faced with the suffering of a newborn infant. But we shouldn't really speak of the tenderness of God yet, because we have still to find it in the text.

What happened on the day of this birth? The description God gives of that day relates above all to actions that were not performed, rather than ones that were. If there is an abomination it is also by omission.

- "Your cord was not tied"; the absence of this action puts the infant in immediate danger of death, as a doctor confirmed to me.

- "You were not washed in water to be cleansed"; whereas the first action, cutting the cord, is not necessarily done with tenderness, the second very likely is. One need only see a mother wash her new-born for the first time to discover the maternal tenderness she deploys, taking delight in stretching the moment out, such is her pleasure in prolonging her contact with her infant.

---

1. In the French the image is always of Jerusalem as feminine; the child is always a little girl. (Trans.)

– "You were not rubbed in salt"; this action is a little mysterious because it receives no other mention in the Bible. Commentators, with the support of non-biblical texts, think it refers to a ritual designed to protect a newborn from the malign influence of demons. Perhaps this was a practice of the Hittites or the Amorites, but we know little of their customs. Clearly it must have been of benefit to the child.

– "You were not wrapped in cloth"; here we have to do not with a vital act but with one that gives a mother opportunity to express all the tenderness she has towards her child.

God deliberately describes these actions, no doubt to emphasize how the life of this infant was compromised, and how deprived of maternal tenderness.

"Nobody looked at you with pity to do one of these things with compassion"; not just the father and the mother but no other person paid any attention to Jerusalem. The words "pity" and "compassion" are redundant and underline the degree to which the suffering of the child now attracts tenderness.

Deliberate Infanticide

There we have everything that was *not* done, all the omissions, the gravity of which had already compromised the life of the infant. God continues his account, relating what was done and fits the description of abomination.

"You were cast out into the field"; this is worse than being left abandoned on a street, where a child can be found and saved; it would have no chance in the fields since, biblically, the fields are the territory of wild beasts. It is most unlikely that the first to come across the infant would be a person, but rather some animal which would devour her. To cast a child out into the fields is to condemn it to death, which is to say that the deliberate intention of the parents of Jerusalem was that the child die. We are speaking of straightforward infanticide. A thousand explanations could be sought to justify or blacken the attitude of the parents, but God puts forward just one, of extreme gravity: "disgust," a disgust or revulsion so profound that the soul itself is its object; "in disgust for your soul."

Not only is this child physically damaged, having been cast out into the fields, but she is wounded to the depths of her being by the revulsion of which she is the object on the part of her own mother and father. This is terrible! It is truly awful to experience this from the day of your birth! About to die! There are no words to describe what the suffering might be of little Jerusalem! Perhaps one might overcome the physical wounding undergone at birth, but how to get past inner wounds experienced from such an early time? The wound of disgusted rejection; this is unfathomable and unspeakable suffering, which leaves its marks on the entire life!

Disgust, rejection; this also has to do with the emotions and is really the opposite of tenderness. Disgust keeps you away; those who are full of it recoil, while tenderness approaches and seeks the softness of touch. In the rejection with which she is surrounded, this infant experiences the opposite of tenderness.

All this is so vile, so nauseating, that God himself makes no effort to find words with which to charge the guilty parties. He contents himself with phrases in the passive to focus attention only on the child—"You were not . . . you were not . . . you were not . . . you were . . ." But why? God is silent about the parents because only the child matters to him!

Abandoned in Disgust

The parents have gone; the abandonment is manifest and must surely lead to death. There are other abandonments described in the Bible, but none as violent as this. I will give an example here which, in its contrast, underscores again the abomination suffered by little Jerusalem.

The book of Genesis tells us the story of Hagar, forced to flee alone into the desert with Ishmael, her child (Gen 21:14–16). After becoming lost in the desert and after exhausting her reserves of water and food, this mother finally abandons her son, leaving him under a bush, and steals away, saying, "That I may not see my son's death." She withdraws to weep in the distance. Yes, we have here an abandonment with the same outlook of death; but the situation is quite different; Hagar was forced to abandon her child and she did it without any violence or any sign of rejection. On the contrary, the tears she sheds speak of maternal tenderness.

Abandonment with tenderness has nothing in common with the abandonment of revulsion!

In terms of literary style, Ezekiel's account describes this day of birth within bookends, that is to say, by repeating an expression at the end used at the beginning. "In the day when you were born" is said at the opening of verse 4; "in the day when you were born," is repeated at the end of verse 5. This bookending has the effect of putting the birth into parentheses as if it was a parenthesis opened and closed within the life of the parents, an episode that can be put to the side and not so much as inscribed on their memories. The birth will also be easier to leave in oblivion given that it took place in the fields without the least witness. The father and mother can leave; neither of them will tell what happened. No one will find out. The wild beasts are to wipe out every trace. It is truly sordid! Nauseating!

An Unseen Witness

However, after this carefully closed parenthesis, everything rebounds. The affair becomes known. The secret can be revealed, simply because an unseen witness suddenly steps forward and now speaks up. "I passed close by you!" The witness is none other than God himself. "I passed close by you and I saw you . . ."

God has passed by, just after the departure of the parents no doubt, and just in time to confirm what anyone would have seen, that the cord was not tied, the infant had not been washed, salted, or clothed, and she bore in her flesh the bruises that showed she had been thrown out. But God sees beyond and what no other witness would have noted, the wounds of rejection left in the depths of the soul! God alone was able to see this; he saw and bears witness to it.

God begins to tell Jerusalem what nobody else could, since there was no other witness; "this is what I saw, my child, when you were in your blood, abandoned in the fields, your soul wounded by disgust . . ."

God's Testimony about Our Life

God is the first witness and it seems the only one, the only one at least who can tell Jerusalem what happened on the day of her birth. God tells it later, after the event, when Jerusalem has long been an adult. What God then says is a real revelation; he reveals to Jerusalem her own history, a history no one could verify, certify, or authenticate . . . a history that has to be received from God by faith alone, with no way of verifying that what he says is correct! Faced with the testimony of God, Jerusalem must now welcome his account in complete faith.

In the Bible, when a witness steps forward to reveal an important fact, or something as serious as the abandonment of a child, it is required that the testimony be corroborated by that of one or two others if it is to be accepted (Deut 17:6). This, of course, is just as necessary today, but here there is only the witness of God, his word alone, to take or leave.

God therefore takes as witness the heavens and earth (Deut 4:26), which is particularly apt because heaven was perfectly placed to assist at this birth, which took place in the open fields, and the earth can also bear witness, the earth that received the infant cast onto its surface. The entire cosmos had been a witness. Nevertheless, while God was able to hear the testimony of heaven and earth, and the whole cosmos could confirm God, who in Jerusalem would have ears attuned enough to hear their witness?

Here then is Jerusalem, ignorant of her own history, but about to hear it from the mouth of God himself. Jerusalem discovers her life in the words of God, who reveals it to her. Just so, the biblical text concerns us to the highest degree; whoever we might be, the one best placed to relate to us our own history is God himself, and it is in the Bible that we can best discover all that can make our lives clear to us. No doubt none of us has experienced just what is described here, but I believe that we all, whatever our story, can find in the Bible clarification, illumination, revelation of what constitutes the real depths of our being. God, better than anyone, makes us understand the secrets of the hidden place because he is the only true witness, the only one who sees right into the heart of our being, sees what escapes the eyes of others, the only one in whom we can have perfect confidence to make things clear. How true this is and how it fills me with wonderment and thanksgiving.

God's Silence about His Feelings

"I passed by and I saw," says God. The order of these verbs awakens in us the memory of a well-known parable that tells the story of several people in a corner just as remote and isolated as the field where Jerusalem was thrown out, a passage about a wounded man, also in mortal danger, a wounded man abandoned by brigands by the side of a road, despoiled of all his goods. Then, the parable tells us, a priest *passed by* the wounded man, *saw* him, but didn't stop; a Levite *passed by*, *saw*, but didn't stop, and then a Samaritan *passed by*, *saw*, but he did stop (Luke 10:33).

I refer to this parable in part because we meet again the two verbs "pass" and "see," but above all because it contains another phrase that makes beautifully clear the attitude of the good Samaritan and the reason for his salutary intervention. "Passing by, the Samaritan saw him and was moved inwardly, with compassion." Jesus carefully details the feelings of the Samaritan in order to explain his attitude—"he was moved inwardly, with compassion." Here, in contrast, seeing little Jerusalem, God tells us that he passed by, that he saw, but he says nothing of his inward feeling, his emotions, nothing of his compassion, nothing of his tenderness. This silence of God about what he sees speaks volumes to us; does he feel nothing for this infant wounded to the core? Or does he conceal his feelings behind an extreme sensitivity? There is a point here we must clarify in our quest into the tenderness of God. Clearly God did not continue on his way as do the priest and the Levite in the parable! He stopped to speak to the infant the extraordinary word, "Live!" But what can we say exactly about God's feelings faced with this little Jerusalem?

Close to the Humble One

If we turn to the story of Hagar and Ishmael, we note that in the Genesis account God hears the cries of the infant, but from heaven (21:17) and not from earth, whereas here God comes much closer; he passes "close by" the infant, at her side, in the field. Wonderful proximity!

In the story of Ishmael, God sends an angel in his place to save the child (21:17). Here, God intervenes directly, and reveals himself as much closer. The presence of Hagar perhaps explains why God doesn't intervene directly in the case of her son. God does not show himself to people, not even to take care of a child because of his reticence and preference to intervene without witness. In the account in Ezekiel the mother is no longer there, and little Jerusalem is alone and still too small to understand the extreme closeness of God as he intervenes on

40

her behalf. He intervenes directly without delegating an angel or an archangel . . . He comes close, wonderfully close!

There is no witness to the passing by of God, not even an angel, so that no one will ever know who tied the cord, who washed the child, who rubbed her with salt, who clothed her. Someone has to have done it, but it is a total mystery! It will only remain where it is, deep in the soul of the child, more deeply imprinted no doubt than the rejection which had already bruised her. But how can we know, when God stays absolutely silent on all this? He is too humble and modest to say anything about what his maternal tenderness had done . . . But forgive me please, reader friend, because I am going too fast, beyond the evidence . . . ! Before supposing this tenderness on God's part we need to go back in the text to a small detail that shows how God could be moved by the child.

Total Silence about Tenderness

To find this detail we will make a comparison with a similar account of an abandoned child, specifically that which tells us how Moses was abandoned by his mother and saved from death by someone who passed by. You know the story, that the abandonment of which Moses was the victim was a forced abandonment; that his mother had no choice but to abandon him, against her wishes, because of a decree of Pharaoh, the tyrant of the time. This mother did all she could to avoid her child's death, sending her daughter to watch over the child. Then someone passes by close to the abandoned child, Pharaoh's own daughter. The account here bears some resemblance to ours; the young girl is "walking" by and "sees" the child and even hears him cry. The text then gives us an important phrase that indicates the ultimate motive of this young girl—"she was moved with compassion" (Exod 2:6).

There is nothing of this in the Ezekiel account! Nothing is said of any compassion this child might awaken but rather we find a striking contrast. "No one," says God, "fixed their eyes upon you with a look of pity that would lead to compassion." Nobody had compassion on you. A little later, God goes on to say, "as for me, I saw you." Yes, God fixes his attention upon the child, but is it a look of compassion? It seems very probable, but that is not what is said; God says nothing about what he felt looking at this bruised newborn. Perhaps it is beyond words, even for him? Perhaps it is extreme reserve?

God's Feelings Give Him Away

A straightforward review of the texts we've examined will help us to understand just when feelings of tenderness are aroused. The Samaritan passes close by the wounded man, sees him, and is moved inwardly; Jesus passes Nain, sees the widow, and is deeply moved; Pharaoh's daughter passes along the bank of the Nile, sees the baby Moses, and is moved with compassion. The process is the same each time: to pass by, to see, to be moved.

What happens here with God? He passes by the infant, he sees her, and how does he react? He reacts in a most surprising way, he repeats himself: "I said to you when you were in your blood, Live! And I said to you when you were in your blood, Live!" This is a curious reaction on which I will dwell for a moment because there is something here in the repetition that may escape our Western sensibility, and which admirably expresses the degree to which God was moved.

This repetition was so little understood by the Greek authors of the Septuagint translation that they only stated the phrase once. We are very much fashioned by Greek thought, and we have to make a special effort to take hold of the value there is in biblical thought of a repetition like this if we are to enter more fully into the text.

When someone is really moved this can manifest itself in repetition when they speak. You will have noticed; emotion can act upon a person so that they stammer, despite themselves. This stammering comes from the difficulty of containing feelings. This human reality is taken into account in the Hebrew and expressed in a most significant way by the repetition of a word or group of words that are particularly charged with emotion. The Hebrew follows this pattern for God himself to show that things work the same way for him; he also is subject to strong emotion, and it may be to the point where he repeats himself, despite himself, no doubt.

Out of reticence God does not say that he was moved, yet his emotions betray him! How marvelous for us that God be overwhelmed by his feelings to the point of being unable to contain them!

Here then we have God faced with this deeply wounded little girl, so moved that he stammers, stumbling over the only word he speaks to her, at the moment when he wishes to return her to life. This feeling is so immediate to God that years later, when he tells Jerusalem the events of her birth, he stammers again, "I said to you when you were in your blood, Live! I said to you when you were in your blood, Live!"

His emotion is so great that God cannot bring himself to continue with the story of the birth. He interrupts his account, in silence no doubt, before continuing, as if fearing that to continue the evocation of the moment would disturb him still more deeply and cause him to stammer again!

Repetition and Emotion

In order to convince you of what I am saying I will give some other biblical examples that demonstrate clearly how repetition can reveal emotion, particularly in the case of God.

A very beautiful example is given us in a passage in Genesis already rich with emotion, the passage that recounts to us the sacrifice Abraham was called upon to make in offering his son, Isaac. This is a particularly powerful story, which deeply moves, to the core, anyone who reads it. Well, at the moment of the most intense emotion, the moment when Abraham has raised his knife to offer his son, a voice from heaven makes itself heard, stopping him and saying, "Abraham! Abraham!" (22:11). The repetition reveals the degree to which God is moved by this poignant situation. He is so moved that he is unable to add another word. God, overcome by emotion!

Another example is given to us in the account of the calling of Samuel, the young child whom his mother consecrated to God, and who was living as a servant to the priest Eli in the sanctuary at Shiloh. On the night when God comes to speak to him for the first time, Samuel, not recognizing the voice of someone who has not spoken to him before, believes that Eli is calling him. The same scene is repeated, then repeated again, which shows us how much Samuel wanted to obey, and also enables Eli to finally understand that the call heard by the child came from God. Then God calls again to this child so disposed to obey, so open and available. This so moves God that at the moment of addressing him he stumbles over the one word that comes to his lips—"Samuel, Samuel!" (1 Sam 3:10). This repetition, followed by silence, shows us how moved God can be by a child who consecrates himself to him.

With Samuel, as with Abraham, and as with little Jerusalem, God seems unable to pursue his purpose, as if he needs time to take a hold of himself and control his emotions. The silence that follows leaves Samuel, like Abraham, time to respond, which no doubt is not the case with little Jerusalem, who was too small to reply! Each time, however, the feelings of God are so strong that he cannot manage to say more than one repeated word.

Further Examples of Repetition

Here is another example in case you are not yet convinced. I take this example from a text that is less powerful but still significant of God's feelings. This is a passage where God addresses his people, who he knows to be in pain and fear. The situation moves God, and he comes to console his people, saying to them, "It is I, it is I who comfort you" (Isa 51:12). God speaks here of his compassion with such feeling that he stumbles over the first word of the phrase. A little earlier in the same book of Isaiah, to the same people who are suffering from having wounded God, God responds with such great mercy that he is seized with emotion as he expresses his pardon; "It is I, it is I who blot out your transgressions" (43:25). Whether it is the tenderness of his compassion or the tenderness of his mercy, God knows what it is to be moved; it is excellent for us to realize that his tenderness is so strong and so true that he may have difficulty controlling his feelings towards those he loves.

I will also give a final example that I find quite extraordinary and that will help us to re-center ourselves in our approach to the mystery of the tenderness of God. This example is found in a text we have already looked at, that in which God says for the first and last time that he is a God of tenderness, Exodus 34. We have seen how God spoke this as a confidence to his friend Moses, with such reserve that he hides himself in a cloud. Now, at the very moment when God reveals his tenderness, he is so moved that he stumbles at the first word he pronounces; and what is so extraordinary is that this first word is none other than his own name, "Adonai, Adonai" (34:6). The actual name of God is not used here as being too holy, but it is indeed this name, the Tetragram (YHWH), which is repeated in God's own mouth. This is the only time in the Bible that God is so moved as to repeat his own name; "the Lord said to Moses, 'Adonai, Adonai, God of tenderness.'"

When the Greeks translated this verse, I don't know whether they found the repetition incongruous or in bad taste, but they suppressed it! I believe that, unfortunately, they did not accord great import to the feelings of God. They erased the feeling of intimacy here in favor of certainty and solemnity. The worst aspect of this is that this translation has profoundly marked Christian theology and, beyond doubt, those who refuse to believe today that God can be moved with emotion.

45

Tenderness Is Action

Emotions are diverse and it is up to us to discern in any passage what feeling might be transmitted in the repetition. Here, in the case of a dying infant, it seems to me that God's emotion is one of compassion. As you know, with God compassion is always tied to tenderness. I believe then that the one word God manages to stammer out to the child is steeped in compassionate tenderness, *"Live!"*

This is not in itself a word of tenderness. It might be spoken in tones other than tenderness and with more or less forcefulness. If the tenderness is there, it is not in the word itself but in the tenderness which God gives it. It is similar to the "don't cry" addressed by Jesus to the widow at Nain. Did God whisper it into the ear of the child? Did he say it with more intensity? I don't know, but I do know that it was spoken in such a way as to enter into the deepest place in the child. No need for a lengthy discourse; just one word from God is enough for all his tenderness to fill the heart of an infant in distress and return her to life, and how good it is that this happened—the child survived thanks to the tenderness of God. How marvelous!

One Word from God

Now, the one word spoken to the child, what exactly was it? In the Hebrew it is enough just to hear it to be overcome with emotion. In Hebrew, the word sounds like this, "Haiee." To our ear it sounds like an onomatopoeia close to the same in every language in the world. In the Hebrew it is a little more guttural than our "Aiee," but the sound alone of the word suffices to convey the pain God feels confronted with this wounded child, as if he feels bad in her place, with her and for her. . . . All his compassion is expressed in the one word and that with redoubled force because the word is repeated: *"Hayî! Hayî!"*

A God suffering in compassion, such is the God who reveals himself here in wonderful fashion. How marvelous it is that this God reveals himself to us, as though secretly, out in the fields, humbly, with no human witness, with such modesty that even the angels and archangels are held at a distance. You should know that I feel overwhelmed with emotion toward this God. . . .

The Very Life of God

"Live!" This is the first word this child has heard in her life. The first, because no one anywhere near had spoken a word since her birth. No one, because her father and mother, seized with revulsion towards her, abandoned her. When someone abandons a child they don't say a word or even make a sound lest the child retain something in its memory, perhaps just the timbre of the voice to which it might become attached. Nothing, not even a word! The heavens and earth are mute with amazement! Not even one word from a passer-by, because there was no one in the fields that day. The first to pass by was God. The first and the only word that this child hears comes from the mouth of God, from the heart of God, out of his tenderness. Nothing more; but this tenderness snatches the child from death and returns her to life. We see how powerful the gentleness of tenderness is. There is nothing weak here! The tenderness of God is so gentle that it can touch this child without any aggravation of pain, and so powerful that it snatches her from death with just one word. Only God has tenderness like this, extreme gentleness and extreme power.

In the book of Ezekiel more than in other books of the Bible, the word "ḥayî," also used as an adjective, is a constant refrain in the mouth of God, who refers to himself as "the Living One" (see 5:11; 14:16, 18, 20, etc.). In a way, in inviting this child to life, God is transmitting something of himself, of his own life, making her participate in his own being. If this child survived it is because she was re-attached to the very life of God, because God gave her his very own life. We find that this child was born twice on that day, the first time, of her mother to a life destined for death, and the second time from the mouth of God to a life with the promise of eternity. It is the same with us; the life we receive from our parents is a life that leads to death, but the life we receive from God leads to eternity.

"Live!" This word engraved forever, deep in the memory of this child, is also engraved forever on the heart of God . . . how wonderful!

When God Prays

"Live!" Do we need to say that the word here is not an adjective but an imperative?

In Hebrew there are two ways to give a command, and not just one as in English. These two ways are the imperative and the jussive, this second being a grammatical term used to designate a verbal form we don't have. To distinguish them some translators render the jussive by the future. "You shall not steal, you shall not murder"; these future forms are to be understood as expressing commands.

The main difference between the imperative and the jussive has a claim on our attention here. The jussive essentially is reserved for the commandments of the Law. The imperative, however, is above all reserved for prayer. When we pray to God, saying, "hear me, take pity, forgive my faults . . ." this would never be the jussive, never a command addressed to God. This would be an offence to God, giving him orders! It is always in the imperative, with humility.

What is wonderful here is that, in addressing Jerusalem, God does not give an order, "Live, I command you!" but addresses to her a prayer, "Live, I plead with you!" The tenderness of God is to be found in the humility of this prayer, and would disappear were we dealing with a commandment.

What is even more remarkable is the way the repetition transforms the prayer into an insistent one, that is to say, more of a supplication. God is pleading with the child, "Live! Live!" I don't know if I am right, but this pleading leads me to imagine God, as if on his knees before this child found on the ground in her blood, so wounded that she can't even be touched unless by this supplication that in its humility reaches her soul, "Live, my little one! Live, I beseech you . . ."

You may be surprised by this suggestion, but I hope you will not be shocked at being told that God might pray to a human being! But it is the Bible that invites me to picture things this way, leading us to understand the degree to which God is humble in his love.

Jesus himself demonstrates this, particularly in the famous Parable of the Prodigal Son, which we have already looked at. He describes the father, in fact, as praying, not to the prodigal, but to his other son, sulking and railing in the fields and shutting himself off from the joy of his father. Jesus tells us that the father went out into the fields to find his son and convince him to come in. "He prayed him to enter," Jesus tells us (Luke 15:28), using a Greek word that roundly and soundly means "pray." Behind the father stands God himself, who pleads with the recalcitrant children that we are. A humble and wonderful God!

The gesture of supplication is "stretching out your hands" towards God, as we see specifically in Psalm 143:6. There is another text in which God, so to speak, reverses the roles, addressing to us these astonishing words, "All day long I have stretched out my hands towards this rebellious people" (Isa 65:2). He is a humble God, who sets himself to entreat, every day, those who are rebellious towards him.

This then is the humble God whose tenderness becomes prayer towards a little dying girl. What a wonder!

The Tender Word That Heals _____

I have described at length the violence of which little Jerusalem was a victim. I have taken this time in order to underline the infinite tenderness that God deploys to heal the effects of this violence on the child.

The violence struck the child on two levels, the physical, in her body, cast out into the fields, and in her soul, through the disgust heaped out upon her. How did God intervene to soothe and heal these wounds to her body and soul? How may we, we too, intervene on behalf of suffering people we draw alongside, who are wounded in their soul, perhaps more than their body? God shows us the way; the only care he lavishes on this child is his tenderness.

His tenderness is expressed in two ways, first of all by his word, by the prayer "live!" he speaks to the child, his supplication overflowing with tenderness. Just as a word can wound, a word of tenderness has the extraordinary power of touching the soul, the wounded soul, without hurting again. The tender word pronounced here by God manages to soothe and heal this half-dead child and lead her back to life. Truly, the tender word is both a caress and a balm for the soul. A soul that has been whipped, wounded, and bruised cannot bear any other contact than the caress of tenderness. When the soul bleeds the only balm that can heal is tenderness.

The Tenderness of a Look _____

Besides speech, and as a complement to speech, there is also the look that God fixes on this child; "I saw you . . . and I said." God's looking, which accompanies and underlies what he says, really comes first. Before speaking, God begins by looking at the child, fixing his gaze upon her. This looking awakens his tenderness, which then fills both his words and his gaze. When a person overflows with tenderness, everything in him becomes that tenderness, both his speech and the look in his eye.

As there are words that wound, sometimes terribly, and others that wonderfully soothe, so there are looks that wound, at times terribly, and others that wonderfully soothe. A look that accompanies words of tenderness can only be a look of tenderness, a look that consoles and comforts; and it is just such a look that God fixes on the wounded child.

A look of tenderness has this about it, that it can be fixed on the physical being without doing harm, a caress. That of God can fasten onto a soul and never hurt. Such is the look of God here, fastening with great gentleness on the bruised body of this child, and also onto her soul, falling upon it like the dew that falls onto the ground.

This child had at first been regarded with loathing by her parents, but is now viewed with tenderness by God. This look, at first silent, has, even before God begins to speak, I believe, cleansed the child better than water or salt, has wrapped the child better than any cloth, has wiped away from her soul every trace of disgusted rejection. But, forgive me, I say too much; I should stop because I am in the midst of what is inexpressible in the text, the silence of tenderness that comes to see through to its end the work begun by the word and the gaze.

The one word pronounced by God on that day sounds on in the silence that follows. The look of tenderness and the word of tenderness flow into a silence that is also full of God's tenderness. Silence indeed is needed to allow time for tenderness to carry its work into the depths of the soul. In this silence God's gaze is unswerving; it remains fixed on the child as she becomes silent. How I wish that every wounded soul on earth could know that the silent gaze of God is fixed upon him or her with an infinite tenderness!

"I saw you struggling"[2]

What is the first thing God saw that awakened his tenderness? The text tells us, "I saw you, struggling in your blood." The verb used in the Hebrew conveyed here by "struggling" is difficult to translate. The Greeks translated it as "soaked" and some translators have followed the Greek; but the Hebrew doesn't really say that.

The primary meaning of the Hebrew word is "kick." It is used here in the reflexive, which suggests in an explicit way the child kicking, as it were, at herself. You can see the child laid on the ground and kicking her legs, kicking in the way all infants do. But how are we to understand here this agitation, this struggling? It can be understood in two contradictory ways, both of which, I believe, express truth. Since we are dealing here with a collective oracle, I think we can apply both meanings because people wounded in their souls react in either one way or the other.

"I saw you kicking at yourself." This infant sees the day in a totally hostile context, everything pushing towards death. There are those in a similar situation, in such hostile surroundings, who begin to desire nothing so much as death. "Because the whole world wants me to die, die is what I will do." We might think then that this infant, pressed towards death, struggles and kicks the better to get what she wants, to hasten death. This dramatic situation of profound despair is discovered by God and moves him to the greatest degree, leading him to say, "Live! Live!" a cry that he calls to the child as if a supplication. This call towards life is the only thing that resonates in the soul of the child when everything around is pushing towards death. "Live"; this plea is heard by the child in the depths of her wounded soul, and she survives! Wonderful tenderness that causes life!

"I saw you struggling." The other way to understand is to see this as an effort towards life, the description of a child who fights against all

---

2. The French is *gigoter*, and suggest the sort of random, vigorous kicking, struggling movements a baby makes. (Trans.)

the odds to survive, against the hostile environment to which she was born, against the death to which her parents had consigned her, against the rejection in which she is drowning. The infant struggles, but like a drowning person who can't swim—a dramatic situation that must lead to despair, a situation God discovers and is moved by to the highest degree, leading him to say, "Live!" a word he throws out like a life buoy that saves a shipwrecked man with no strength from drowning. And the child embraces this prayer cast into the deep place of her soul, and survives. Wonderful tenderness which causes life!

The Mediation of the Prophet

We can place ourselves in the sixteenth chapter in Ezekiel in two ways and interpret it accordingly, either by putting ourselves in the place of the little girl, or the person to whom God first addresses himself, that is to say, the prophet Ezekiel. In fact, the text begins in this way; "The word of the Lord was addressed to *me* in these words . . ." The one who expresses himself in this way is Ezekiel, who is charged with the transmission of the oracle to Jerusalem. It is he who God calls upon first, and, curiously, the vocative by which he calls him is not his own proper name, Ezekiel, but less specifically, "son of man," which may also decidedly include us, being as we are, children of men. Understood and received in this sense, the text makes us into messengers. We receive, therefore, the mission from God to pass on to others his message of tenderness. And what could our calling be as Christians other than to proclaim this good news?

"Son of man, make known to Jerusalem these words. You shall say to them . . ." It is this that God requires of us, to go and tell all the little Jerusalems that we encounter and who endure similar suffering, to tell what the heart of God is towards them, his marvelous tenderness.

So it is that God charges people with transmitting his message of tenderness. He charges them with an extraordinary mission, to speak of what is to be found in the heart of God, of his mystery, of his infinite love, of what would otherwise be incomprehensible, it goes so far beyond us and is so distant from all that we are, so removed from our inadequate human love, our second-rate human tenderness. How poor we are! There is a chasm between the heart of God and our human heart! How should we speak? What can we say?

It is good that we recognize that this is how things are, but while it may all be true, God nevertheless tells us that the message is addressed to people, concerns people, and is designed to touch the hearts of people. Isn't it better that people be addressed by people? Who better than a human can speak to a human? So here is something more we can take from this text—"Go, son of man, and speak to others; you will understand the story of this little girl; it is a very human story, awfully human even. You will understand her because you, you also, have the heart of a human, the insides of a human. You will know how to find the human words to speak to people and tell them of my tenderness towards them. You will know how to find the human tones of voice that must accompany the human words of this oracle, the tones that will touch the human ear, because your voice, better than mine, knows the correct chord to touch the human ear and heart. You will know how to speak because those you speak to, you love and know; they have in their veins the same blood that flows through yours, while I, I am God and not a human; I don't have a human heart or the guts of a man! The truth is, you are closer to them than I am. Go then, son of man, it is to your brothers and sisters in humanity that you are to speak . . ."

God doesn't speak directly to Jerusalem, but he commands Ezekiel to do so. Ezekiel was a priest in the temple in Jerusalem, so he was particularly well placed to address the inhabitants of the city of which he is a part and for which he is responsible. In a sense, he is more of a Jerusalemite than is God himself. You see, reader friend, how effectively we are involved in the text; it makes us God's messengers, messengers specifically authorized to pass on words that concern to the utmost degree our brothers and sisters.

Whoever receives the oracle in this way, and feels bound to assume this mission as a messenger, cannot but feel and take account of his own inadequacy, his nakedness, his nothingness and unworthiness faced with such a task. For this reason he must take time to turn to God, stretching out his hands and saying, "My Lord and my God, have pity on me; you see the extent to which I am incapable and unworthy of such a mission. If in your grace you have found it good to send me, with my humanity, then I beg you—in your grace, and by your Holy Spirit—be sure to impart to my love the warmth of yours, to my words the wisdom of yours, to my look the gentleness of yours, to my tenderness the delicacy and strength of yours; be sure to mold me in the depths of my heart, my soul, my belly, so that I don't betray, pervert, or obscure anything that comes from you."

It is not only good to pray this way before catapulting yourself into the highways and byways, but to pray like this the full length of the road.

This said, as we become messengers of the oracle of God, we discover two gifts. Above all, the great trust that God places in us. It is as if he says to us, "Go, I have no one else to transmit these words to others! I put my word in your heart and in your mouth. Everything depends on you now . . . ." It is an extraordinary and terrible trust.

The other thing we find is the extreme humility of God, who regards us as closer to men than he is, even he who fashioned man and who in truth knows them much better. God very humbly effaces himself behind us his messengers. And what a demand this makes for humility on our part if we are to testify of such a humble God!

"Son of man, you will say . . ." Here, we are sent by God to speak to the wounded; but before we launch ourselves into human society to accomplish our mission, we need to take time to go more deeply into the Scripture so we can understand it and pass it on more effectively.

A Little Pagan

If this child was the object of so much revulsion on the part of her parents, we should also recognize that there is plenty to have inspired the same response in God. However, there is nothing of that in him. God doesn't evince the slightest revulsion towards this child and on the contrary is filled with infinite tenderness; but we should also bear in mind how almost incomprehensible this tenderness is, because, all things considered, there is plenty about the child that might well produce disgust in God.

What then, you will say, is there that could inspire this revulsion in God? It's that the child is a little pagan, not a descendant of Abraham, and as such is a child under a curse, and entirely impure. A pagan, cursed and impure; there is enough here to repel God and cause revulsion in him. We will dwell a little on these points.

First of all, though, the very fact that God might experience disgust may seem impossible to us. But it is certainly possible; he himself says, for example, to his own people the following verse, "My soul will abhor you (hold you in disgust) if you do not listen to me" (Lev 26:30). Here we have God evincing disgust, but also capable of surmounting it, happily for us.

This child is a little pagan, as we learn from the mouth of God himself, who names her parents—and if he goes to the trouble of giving these details, it is certainly worth knowing. "Your father was an Amorite and your mother a Hittite." These two nations, in the Bible, are pagan nations, both descendants of Canaan, the pagan (Gen 10:15–16). Descended from such a father and mother, this little one is altogether a pagan.

The Amorite and the Hittite _____

I will indulge in a few remarks here since these two names are mentioned by God. As you know, in Hebrew, proper names are of great importance, each name expressing a deep reality about the one who bears it. We, who often give children names whose meanings we are ignorant of, have rather lost this point of view today, but in the Bible each name conveys meaning.

The father, then, is an Amorite. The word "Amorite" comes from a root, *āmar*, which means "to speak." This girl is the daughter of a man given the gift of speech, the daughter of a man who should have spoken, but did not. At the birth of a child a father is supposed to speak, and has two basic things to say. It is he who is supposed to name the child, give the child a name; but he didn't do it. It is also he who is supposed to pronounce a blessing on the child; but he didn't do it. The disgust he felt towards his daughter no doubt impelled him to abandon her without naming her or blessing her. Such a father is unworthy to be a father, and unworthy even to be an Amorite.

The only one here who utters a word addressed to the child is God. It's remarkable to notice that the verb *āmar* is used to introduce the tender words that proceed from the mouth of God—"I saw you and I said (*āmar*) to you." What he says sounds like a true blessing— "Live!" Here is the true father! When the unworthy father fails in his task and decamps into the distance, God steps forward as one who is perfectly worthy to be a father, a father indeed full of tenderness.

As for the mother, we are told that she is a Hittite. The name of this nation derives from a root *hātat*, which means "to terrorize." If the father was unworthy of his name, the mother is worthy of hers! The revulsion within her towards her daughter has something terrorizing for the soul of the little one. Surely she fits the name well, but the name does not make her unworthy to be a mother. Hittites as well, every mother is made for tenderness and not for revulsion towards her children. She may terrorize those around her, her neighbors, even her husband, but not her children.

To this little one, branded by the revulsion of the woman who brought her into the world, God steps forward with his motherly feelings, his womb-like tenderness, and fills the role of a true mother, saying what every mother is bound to say to her child, "Live!"

"My mother and father may forsake me; but the Lord will take me up." This verse from the Psalms admirably sums up the situation (Ps 27:10).

A Cursed Child

Not only is Jerusalem a little pagan, but she is also cursed. What leads me to say this? It is enough to recall her Amorite and Hittite parentage and you will understand. Both are descendants of Canaan, the son of Ham. You will know that Noah had three sons, Shem, Ham, and Japheth; and you will also know that when he left the ark after the flood, Noah thought it a good idea to celebrate the flood's conclusion and in so doing had more than enough to drink! (Gen 9:21). Noah fell to the ground so drunk that he exposed himself under the effects of the alcohol, which led to his son Ham mocking him. When Noah recovered his senses and learned what had happened, he cursed Ham and with him all his descendants, a curse passed through the generations and reaching both the Hittites and the Amorites. By inheritance, then, little Jerusalem is well and truly cursed, from birth.

An Impure Child

Not only is she pagan and cursed, but impure as well. This is heavily underlined by God himself who speaks three times of the blood in which the child is covered. "I saw you struggling in your blood, and I said to you while you were in your blood, 'Live!' I said to you while you were in your blood, 'Live!'" In the Bible the blood is a source of impurity. This is why it was so necessary to wash the newborn, which was not done, as God states. "You were not washed in water to be cleansed."

Tenderness Greater Than Revulsion

Here then is this little one, with everything against her from her birth, everything that might be rejected by God and repulsed in disgust; she is pagan, cursed, and impure. This representation of the child strongly underscores the astonishing miracle that, instead of walking away in disgust, God draws near in tenderness. Everything about him is tenderness as soon as he sees this little child. What a surprising and marvelous tenderness, altogether unexpected!

The energy God invests in this child is pure grace. A further comment can be added to underline again how the attitude of God is all grace. When God passes by the child she does nothing but kick. There is no crying or complaining and we know how sensitive God is to the cry of infants (Exod 2:23–24); he hears such cries as a prayer of the Holy Spirit (Rom 8:22–26). There is a beautiful Jewish tradition that considers the first cry of a newborn as heard and regarded by God as a prayer. Little Jerusalem doesn't cry or complain, does nothing that resembles a prayer meriting the tenderness of God. Here it is truly grace.

Once more this extraordinary tenderness of God has nothing weak about it. The tenderness is stronger than human cursing, stronger than ancestral and even patriarchal cursing. It is stronger than social and even racial prejudices, stronger than any human revulsion. Such again is the paradox of tenderness, so strong in its gentleness.

I find this text altogether amazing; it moves me profoundly to think that this marvelous tenderness of God concerns all of us, everyone. It grabs me each time I hear someone speak of their life in terms that perhaps strongly resemble those described here.

You know, this text concerns every child who was not loved, every abandoned child, every child deprived of tenderness, all those uncared for and who have been a source of disgust to those around them, all the little pagans, cursed or unclean who have been cast out, into the fields perhaps, but also under bridges and on pavements, where there are other savage beasts who watch for them as if for prey. These children are innumerable, and they later become adults who continue to carry around inside themselves the child they were, and still suffer from the rejection of which they were the object, a rejection so profound that it often turns to self-rejection.

Reader friend, I often encounter people like this and you are sure to as well. To everyone, really everyone, each time the opportunity arises I try as best I may to tell what is in this text, the unbelievable and wonderful tenderness of God, of which no one is worthy but which nevertheless fills the heart of God to the point of enveloping everyone equally and causing us to live. I can't believe there is any situation more painful, more desperate, more abhorrent than that described here. And though there may never have been a person in greater suffering than little Jerusalem, should such a person come to see you, then, reader friend, son of man that you are, I believe that you can say to them: "You, who have known nothing but rejection and contempt, who have never known tenderness, you who believe yourself unclean and unworthy of God, who think that death alone can offer you a welcome, know that the rejection that sickens you is not in the heart of God towards you; know that the tenderness you know nothing of is in the heart of God and it is for you; know that his look of tenderness is fixed on you and that you are wrapped up in it to make you live; know that there is nothing more beautiful for you than this tenderness, which rests upon all your sufferings as a balm. To you also God says with all the gentleness and all the strength of his tenderness, which he addresses to you as a prayer, 'Live, I plead with you! Live, my child!'"

This is not a question of denying what life can be, suppressing the facts, white-washing them or sweetening them. It's not a question of finding excuses or extenuating circumstances. It's not a matter of hiding from the painful truth of human life, but of affirming something much greater, which brings life when everything impels towards death. It's a matter of speaking the truth of God, the truth of his tenderness, which is gentler and stronger than everything, stronger than any rejection, any contempt, any revulsion, and is able to heal all the wounds of the soul, even those of the soul that is pagan, cursed, and unclean.

Perceiving the Tenderness of God

"Live!" God says, and the child survives. This tells us the power of a tender word, the power that brings life when no life is possible. But it also tells us that the child reacted to what she heard and that she was able to perceive the tenderness spoken to her, that she was sensitive and responded. This poses an immense question about our capacity to perceive the tenderness of God. What exactly is it?

The text shows us clearly that we are able from birth to perceive the tenderness of God, whether believers like us, or, since this child was pagan, non-believers. It shows us that *all* people are able to perceive the tenderness of God, even the most pagan, the most unclean, and even the cursed. I believe the text is clear on this point.

If we are all able to perceive the tenderness of God, how do we do so? Here again the text is very instructive. Given her age, it is clear that this child has not absorbed it by use of her reason, not yet awakened; not by her conscience, as yet undeveloped; nor by her will, which is still in the sleep of birth. Nevertheless, in telling us of this birth, God tells us that the child did perceive his tenderness without revealing just how she perceived it. There is here a great mystery which we have to leave as such, a mystery, without seeking to penetrate it more deeply. I will just say instead, quite simply, that this child, like each of us, experiences this tenderness with every fibre of her being, in the deepest parts, in what Hesychius of Batos terms "the inaccessible depths of the soul"

(*On Vigilance* 22). I love this particular expression of Hesychius, which specifies that these depths are inaccessible to our intellects, but not to the tenderness of God. How wonderful to know!

The child survives, it is a fact; the inaccessible depths of the soul, though encrusted with rejection, do not prevent her from knowing the tenderness of God. This leads us to say simply, it seems to me, that the soul was already able to know this divine tenderness even when confused by rejection, so this capacity is innate, inherent to the very nature of the human heart. I believe that every soul has the capacity to welcome this tenderness; that it is a constituent of the human being since the time of creation, so that every person is predisposed to live by this tenderness.

The Soul Fashioned by the Tenderness of God

I feel able to say this because I believe that it is implicitly stated in the biblical account of the creation of humanity. The account reveals that after fashioning man out of the dust of the earth, God "breathed into his nostrils the breath of life and he became a living being" (Gen 2:7). This verse says that the soul issues from the breath of God, from the breath of his mouth, from the light, slight, and quiet inrush of air with the breath breathed into his nostrils. I believe that this gentle breath of God is full of tenderness and that the soul proceeds out of the tenderness of the breath of God, which is why it is so sensitive to this tenderness which gave it life. It is enough, then, for God to call this little Jerusalem into life, to call her while still wounded, to call her with tenderness, for her to welcome this tenderness with every fibre of her being and turn to life.

This capacity of the human soul to perceive the tenderness of God is so deeply inscribed upon it that it naturally resists every aggression, every wounding, even the most monstrous rejection; this is so among all people, even the most pagan, cursed, and impure; the soul is awoken from the time God first fixes his tender regard upon her and he speaks over her the word of life.

Here then is this child who responds to the tenderness of God, but the response itself is not described. It is only realized after the event, because the child grows and becomes an adult, but her first reaction to the divine tenderness is passed over in silence; we are again in a mystery that cannot be expressed. We can say the same of our own lives since, like this child, we live in the tenderness of God without knowing how, not even knowing how we responded from our earliest years; it is beyond our memory and consciousness, deposited within the inaccessible depths of our soul. If we do know, it is only because God reveals it to us as he here reveals it to Jerusalem. If we know, it is the fruit of our faith in God's word; if we make it our own, it is by faith. Whether we feel it or not, it is by faith that we know and live in the tenderness of God; it is the knowledge of faith.

Conscious Perception of the Tenderness of God

If, by faith, we can say that we know the tenderness of God, even without feeling it in a conscious way, is it possible, nevertheless, for us to perceive it consciously? And if this is not given to everybody, can it indeed be given, if only to some?

Well, the Bible responds positively to this question, giving us examples of people who do consciously perceive something of God's tenderness. However, it is not with this text in Ezekiel that we need to proceed because this text does not concern an individual in particular but a group of people, a city, the whole of Jerusalem. We can't lean on a collective text if we are to speak of the experience of individuals; a group doesn't necessarily feel what an individual feels.

Jeremiah describes for us how he himself, one particular day in his life, experienced the tenderness of God. It is not God who tells us

63

of this but Jeremiah; he is the one who tells us what he found, what he experienced consciously, his experience of God's tenderness. He tells us of it many dozens of years later, which indicates how it was engraved on his conscious memory.

What Jeremiah recounts took place early in his life, and concerns what was, no doubt, his first conscious contact with God, the first encounter inscribed on his memory, an ineffaceable memory. He tells us of it in the opening page of his book (Jer 1). On that day he was, he tells us, still a child or youth (v. 6), and that God called him to make him a prophet to the nations (v. 5). There was a quite understandable reaction on the part of the youth to this wide-ranging mission—fear! God, then, faced with the fearful young man, does all he can to reassure him. This he does with words, saying to him, "Fear not!" (v. 8); but also by means of a gesture, which judging by its calming effect, must have been full of tenderness. The gesture was imprinted on Jeremiah's heart and he describes it himself; "The Lord reached out his hand and touched my mouth" (v. 9). What a wonder! What a marvelous gesture to quieten a frightened lad! Jeremiah was so moved by this action that he takes time to develop what he says, as if to underline the importance the gesture had for him; he might have said simply, and it would have sufficed, "he touched my mouth," but he adds the detail, "he stretched out his hand and touched my mouth." Yes, this is wonderful tenderness that knew just what was needed to quieten the youth.

"The Lord stretched out his hand and touched my mouth," says Jeremiah, but then does not go on to say anything further. He is silent, reassured by the caress of God on his mouth, and is entirely attentive to God who speaks to him.

Pure Grace

This text in Jeremiah is very instructive. It makes it very clear that actions of this nature are not given on the basis of any merit but only through the sheer grace of God. "I chose you from your mother's belly" (v. 5), God says, before giving him this sign of tenderness. "Even before you were formed in your mother's womb"; Jeremiah had nothing to do with it, with God's manifestation of tenderness, which is truly an act of his grace.

The sensitivity of Jeremiah to the tenderness of God is not the fruit of long discipline, the result of a lengthy spiritual walk, which would make it a consequence of human endeavor. No, Jeremiah experiences this action of God not at the end of his spiritual life, but right at its start, when there had been no particular preparation. It all comes from God.

The action is not the conclusion of a spiritual mission, but is the introduction, to prepare him for it.

Though it is a gesture made towards a youth, there is nothing weak about it; on the contrary, it is made to arm, to fix, to prepare the youth for a tough, hard, painful life which is described in the verses that follow in very martial terms. His life would indeed be one of combat. Once more, the gentleness of tenderness is full of strength.

The gesture would never be repeated in Jeremiah's life, but the force of it would pursue its work in him throughout his life, even if at times unknown to Jeremiah; it would be enough for Jeremiah in the future to remember the gesture of divine tenderness for him to realize again the reality of its power.

Faithful Tenderness

The tenderness of God is not ephemeral and has nothing of the passing emotions that are incident to humanity. Media today make great play on the fleeting tenderness of people. Television, for example, knows how to awaken the emotions through images of violence, but the impressions are brief and soon buried and forgotten; television knows we are little inclined to serious engagement. There is nothing of this with

God, whose faithful engagement is total; God is well able to persevere in his tenderness. He is seen here speaking with an oracle to Jerusalem concerning her birth, speaking to her dozens of years later, telling her the story with the same emotion as the first day. The tenderness of God is eternal. The God who is moved with maternal tenderness on the day of her birth and then with loving tenderness towards her as an adolescent, retains his tenderness towards her years later at the conclusion of the oracle: "I will remember my covenant with you, that which I made in the days of your youth; I will make it an eternal covenant" (16:60).

The proof of this eternal fidelity is given us at the close of the book of Revelation when we see appear, at the end of the ages, the city of Jerusalem, decked out as a bride, the well-beloved of God (Rev 21).

A Wounded God

Between these times, between these two great signs of paternal and conjugal tenderness and the proof that this tenderness is eternal, many things took place. While God stayed perfectly faithful, his well-beloved showed herself to be shamefully unfaithful in her love towards God. She went outrageously astray, to the point of prostituting herself. All this is the content of the great oracle of chapter 16, and it helps us better understand the role of Ezekiel; the oracle is a sort of audit that God makes and wishes to make known to Jerusalem through the prophet, at a time when the ignominies and abominations of the unfaithful spouse have become his central concern; God lets the extent of his suffering be known, the extent to which he has been hurt by his well-beloved. We are to understand that God, so grieved, does not wish to give a direct outlet to the pain that overwhelms him.

Is this to say that God's tenderness can be wounded? God does not exactly say so. Be that as it may, in order not to let anything appear openly on this subject, he goes to work discreetly, behind the scenes, making Ezekiel his confidant; "Go, son of man, go and tell my well-beloved her abominations! Go and tell her what is so hard for me to say. Go and pass on the message that I entrust to you, even if you have to add your own words. You will know how to speak what I feel bad about saying in my great pain. Go after my well-beloved . . . !" God hides his wounded tenderness carefully and instructs a third party to speak in his place; Jerusalem will hear nothing directly from the mouth of God, but will hear everything by the mouth of the prophet sent to her. Towards Jerusalem, who doesn't hear from God directly, towards her, God is silent, but what a silence! It is the silence of a grieved God, the silence of his wounded tenderness. It is this silence that still today so often sounds in our ears. This is something we need to know how to understand, questioning, as we so often are, of God's disturbing silence. God is silent when he is hurt. We need to know this, as it can be very enlightening for each of us, for the church, for the whole of humanity.

I said previously that God carries and envelops the child in tenderness and silence, and that he carries us the same way, us too; but it should also be emphasized that it is in the silence of a wounded tenderness that we are carried and wrapped.

Who will reveal to us this wounded tenderness of God when God does not even speak of it exactly to Ezekiel in this oracle?

Jesus and Jerusalem

Jesus also one day passed close by Jerusalem, a long time after the city's day of birth, long after her espousals to the Lord, and a long time indeed after all the abominations described in the book of Ezekiel. He goes past, "he draws near," Luke tells us and "he saw the city" (19:41). How did he react when he saw the city? "He wept!" Luke says. This is so unexpected. How much discreet suffering there is in the simplicity of this word; "Jesus wept over her."

Why did he weep over Jerusalem when he had never wept over other towns, when all were, no doubt, equally blameworthy? He wept because there was a unique bond between him and the city, a bond which is that of the profound love that God has for her, a bond forged in the tenderness of God for the city. God's tenderness for Jerusalem is alive in Jesus; and this tenderness is wounded, which is why he weeps; God's pain is his pain; God's tenderness is his tenderness. Jesus reveals this to us, Jesus who incarnates the divine tenderness, not through a speech, but by tears alone. Would not these tears of Jesus be the very tears of God . . . ?

The tears of Jesus are heavy with the pain felt by God through the centuries, allusively evoked in the oracle of Ezekiel; it is the pain of knowing that what Jerusalem received from her parents, she has inflicted in her turn on her children. Her parents wanted her death, and now she hands over her children to death, offering them in sacrifice to her lovers (v. 20). She gives her children as victims to the abominations of which she was a victim. This is a terrible human reality, which caused God to say, "As was the mother, so is the daughter; you are the daughter of your mother" (v. 44). But God does not just stand idly by before this fact; to the terrible human reality, he opposes the extraordinary reality that issues from within—his compassionate tenderness has not disappeared, but is transformed into an extraordinary merciful tenderness which will be the final word of God in this oracle. "I will pardon everything you have done" (v. 63).

I believe that God, in the end, through the course of the centuries and in the many facets of his tenderness, has not ceased to say the same. "What I said to you when you were innocent in your blood—'Live!'—I say to you now when you have blood on your hands—'Live.'" He says this to her in the tears of Jesus, "I say to you today when my blood is about to flow for you, 'Live!'"

How unfathomable are the depths of faithfulness in this tenderness which is nonetheless pained!

Reader friend, amongst all the wounded beings to be found on the earth, there also we find Christ, quietly present at their side. We mustn't ever forget this! The gospel invites us to always remember that we must go and speak to all the wounded souls, to strengthen or bring comfort to them.

This episode in the life of Jesus causes us to discover something more, as we realize that on this occasion he doesn't instruct a disciple, an intermediary, a prophet, any third person to go and tell Jerusalem of his pain. He addresses himself *directly* to her, saying, "If only you had known in this day that you had been visited . . ." For the first time, Jerusalem hears the pain of God, not from a messenger, but directly, from him, the one she hurts, but who loves her.

The Paradox of Tenderness

All the foregoing is so that we may really be aware that the tenderness of God can be wounded, that it is vulnerable, exposed, handed over to men. The tenderness of God is exposed, deliberately, in all its weakness.

Here we are again, deep in the paradox of the divine tenderness. We see the great power, indeed the Almighty power of a tenderness able to resuscitate the dead.

We see this same tenderness appearing in its extreme fragility, its extreme vulnerability, able to be deeply wounded by the infidelity of human love. I don't believe we have the right to mishandle this paradox by amputating one of its elements. It is true that the tenderness of God is "All-mighty," but it is also truly "All-weak." To deny either of these realities is to misrepresent the tenderness of God. We should hold on to both, because the truth of God's tenderness includes and exceeds both, in a mystery to be contemplated rather than explained. Such is the tenderness of the Father, revealed by the Son and given by the Holy Spirit for us to contemplate in silence, in the infinite and wonderful depth of its mystery.

Jesus Wept

I would like to close this chapter with a patristic text that is very sober, strong, and poignant; it comes from a church father who meditated these tears of Jesus, with constant reference to Ezekiel 16 (above all verses 9 to 13). It evokes the incomprehensible human folly of the wounds we inflict on divine tenderness. It is a text from a Syrian father of the fourth century, Ephraim of Nisibis. I leave it with you without any commentary, needing none. I hope it feeds you in the quietness of meditation.

The daughter of Zion sees the Son
And she hardens her heart!
The Father of mercy pours out his blessing upon her
And she will heap hatred on the Only Son!
The Father had washed her of the blood that covered her
And she will soil the Son with spittle!
He had clothed her with precious fabric and embroidered cloth
And she will dress the Son with a cloak of derision!
He placed a crown upon her head
And she will tress him with a crown of thorns!
He had fed her with fine flour and honey
And she will give him gall!
He had given her the best of wine
And she will hand him a vinegar-soaked sponge!
He brought her into his cities
And she will drag him out of town!
He shod her in fine leather sandals
And she will make him march barefoot to Golgotha!
He had adorned her with a linen belt
And she will pierce his side with a spear!
Then Jesus looked at the city and his tears began to flow.

From the *Commentary of Diatessaron*, SC 121, p. 313.
Each of the first lines recalls Ezekiel 16:6–13.

CHAPTER 3

Merciful Tenderness

(Jeremiah 31:18–20)

Compunction

WE HAVE COME INTO the presence of God who is grieved in his tenderness, not by just anyone but by his well-beloved, even by we who know ourselves to be the beneficiaries of his great tenderness. As we become aware of having hurt God, how should we react if not by suffering ourselves for having acted in such a way? This pain of ours, and of whoever has the feeling of having hurt God, has a very specific name, one that may perhaps be new to you but that it is good to know since it is a helpfully precise term; I speak of compunction. It would be good to stop here in order to better understand our experience when faced with the wounded tenderness of God.

Compunction, the dictionary tells us, is the pain of having wounded the heart of another, and more to the point, the pain of having hurt the loving heart of God. Whoever loves God and realizes that they have hurt him is seized with compunction, that very particular pain at the level of the heart; this is no surprise since it is at the level of the heart that we experience the essence of any love relationship. How does God behave towards compunction, towards people in pain because they have grieved him? Will he merely withdraw in silence?

The word compunction in English is very appropriate because it contains the idea of a puncture, which exactly expresses the Greek word *katanussesthai*, depicting the pain of stabs to the heart. This is a good way of putting it since the heart feels that it has been pierced a thousand times—when it suffers compunction.

The Greek word is very rare in the New Testament (just occurring once), and relatively rare in the Greek version of the Old (fifteen times), but the idea is nevertheless there as an undercurrent in plenty of texts. Many of the Psalms are prayers spoken under compunction, whether the word is present or not. I am sure that your prayers are also often filled with compunction, whether or not it's a word you use!

The New Testament text that uses the word is in the Acts of the Apostles and is most illuminating for us. This passage in fact describes the reaction of the crowd following Peter's lengthy discourse, which opens their eyes, revealing that they have done nothing less than murder the Son of God when they crucified Jesus Christ. This is an open offence that could not but wound God deeply. Understanding the gravity of their action the crowd were "cut to the heart" (2:37). What did these people, cut to the quick, have to say next? "What shall we do?" Without equivocation Peter replies, "Repent!"

This is wonderfully clear; compunction leads naturally to repentance. If God is hurt, there is nothing else to be done but to seek his pardon. Compunction and repentance are inseparable, and to them God will respond in his mercy; which is to say, as you know, he responds from his inner mercy, with his merciful tenderness, drawing on the mercy in his inward parts.

It is compunction that animates the prodigal son on his homeward path, suffering not because of having committed acts contrary to morality, but from having hurt his father's love and even, as Jesus says, having hurt heaven, that is God, just as much as his own father. God is also present to the heart of this son, as a God who has been hurt. "My father, I have sinned against heaven and against you!" (Luke 15:18)

Jesus gives us here a fine detail of truth; to have hurt a loved one is to hurt God at the same time!

After these introductory remarks we will look at the following beautiful text from Jeremiah which he transmits to us here (Jer 31:18–20) as the word of God.

> ¹⁸ I hear the lament of Ephraim. "You have chastised me and I have been chastised like an untrained bullock. Cause me to return and I will return, because you are the Lord my God. ¹⁹ After being turned, I repent; and after recognizing my faults, I strike myself on the thigh, because I am ashamed and confused, because I bear the shame of my youth." ²⁰ Is Ephraim for me a cherished son? A child in whom I delight? The more I speak of him, the more fondly I think of him; I am inwardly moved in his favor; I will show him all my tenderness. The oracle of the Lord.

This is a short text in comparison with the long sixteenth chapter of Ezekiel and also with many of the oracles in Jeremiah. The oracle is indeed one of the shortest in Jeremiah; this is quite simply, it seems to me, because God is particularly moved, and that not by just any emotion. Anger, for example, is also an emotion, but it makes people very forward and talkative; angry people pour out floods of words. There is none of that here. God is overcome by an emotion that stops his mouth, so to speak, an emotion that is easy to identify when we see that the oracle closes with the word that states what it is; "I will show him all my tenderness." God here pronounces the word that, in a manner of speaking, caused him to stammer when he spoke it to Moses—"The Lord, the Lord, the God of tenderness." Here, with Jeremiah, God doesn't stumble in his words, but he has some trouble getting to the point of what he wishes to say. Perhaps he had other things to say, but simply to have pronounced the word "tenderness" seems to stop him in his tracks.

Jeremiah the Confidant _____

This oracle comes from the very mouth of God. It contains words spoken by Ephraim, but this does not mean we are concerned with a dialogue between God and Ephraim. "I hear the lament of Ephraim," God says; he does nothing more than quote Ephraim; he reports the words that he heard and turns them over in his mind. This is then a monologue on God's part in which he repeats what he has heard (vv. 18–19), and then continues by revealing his reactions (v. 20). It is a monologue spoken, no doubt out loud, before Jeremiah so that he will hear it, but without speaking to him directly. It *is* a monologue; God does not address Ephraim directly by referring to him as "you," but only speaks of him in the third person, as "he." In fact, Ephraim will not hear what God says of him. He will not hear God tell him of his tenderness unless Jeremiah undertakes to report to Ephraim what he has heard about him.

Jeremiah appears as a third party between God and Ephraim, a go-between chosen by God himself to be a party to his tenderness towards Ephraim. We find here with Jeremiah what we also discovered with Moses and Ezekiel, that is to say, that God, on occasion, takes people as witnesses to whom he will reveal something of the tenderness he feels towards others, as he does for them too. He makes them a party to what his reserve restrains him from saying directly. Like Moses and like Ezekiel, Jeremiah is taken into God's confidence.

Moses, Ezekiel, Jeremiah . . . there are other confidants in the history of God's people; it seems that God habitually chooses confidants as intermediaries through whom to speak to his people about his tenderness. It is a wonderful modesty, which God does not seem to wish to relinquish. We should be thankful that generation after generation he has given us such confidants of his tenderness; if there were only one per generation that would amply suffice. May he enable us to discern the presence of anyone who carefully testifies to his tenderness in their teaching—or just by laying on their knees the head of a sleeping brother . . .

Those whom God chooses as confidants are those sufficiently sensitive to his tenderness to know that they have to speak of it with the greatest possible delicacy, being very careful with the divine tenderness not to betray or debase or sentimentalize it. Along this line, Jeremiah was a wonderful confidant, one who from a very young age understood that the tenderness of God could be expressed in the intonation of a "do not fear," or by the simple gesture of a hand touching his mouth.

If it is a good thing that a confidant be close to God, to grasp, so to speak, the ungraspable, to read in the heart of God what God so modestly is saying, to understand him by the intonations of his voice and in his silences, it is also good that a confidant be close to those God sends him to, those he is to address; it is good that he be made of the same stuff as them, with the same blood as them in his veins, as we saw with Ezekiel. This is the case here; Jeremiah may not have belonged to the tribe of Ephraim, but he was very close since he was of the tribe of Benjamin, which was not only a neighbor but more or less a sister tribe; Ephraim was a son of Joseph and brother to Benjamin. Like Ephraim, Jeremiah was a descendant of Rachel, who had just been invoked in the previous oracle (vv. 15–17). This kinship tie with Ephraim allows Jeremiah to convey this oracle with all the strength of a love relationship. To speak of the tenderness of God to others it is really necessary to feel a sense of communion with them, to speak their language, to vibrate in harmony with them.

You will have understood that Ephraim does not refer to some one person, but a tribe. As with Jerusalem in Ezekiel 16, we are dealing with a collective oracle.

A Silent Confidant

In receiving this oracle, Jeremiah does not engage in any commentary; he is careful not to add anything, of any sort, or to introduce his own reactions. When he does, elsewhere, have something to say to God, he is very free with his speech, taking liberties that border on insolence or blasphemy, as we see for example in 4:10, where he reacts in his reply as few servants would ever dare. What he says to God in response to an oracle he is invited to transmit is this: "Ah, Lord God, you have cheated this people in speaking of peace when the sword is threatening their lives!" This requires some daring! You would need to feel close to God, even intimate, to speak to him in this tone. It is out of love for his people and love for God that Jeremiah speaks like this, in pain and compassion for his people; he is not braving the thunderbolts of heaven! It's the speech of a man sensitive to the suffering of his people and who knows himself listened to by God with love.

Here, when he receives this short oracle about Ephraim, Jeremiah keeps complete silence, and contents himself with adding, after God's last word, the simple, "Oracle of the Lord," like a signature that authenticates everything he has heard.

What is there here that prevents Jeremiah from reacting or adding any comment? It is, surely, because he hears God trembling with emotion as he speaks of his tenderness, but also, no doubt, because he understands him to be speaking in terms never before heard from the mouth of God; in particular there is one truly unheard-of word that is so surprising it still reduces us to silence today. Jeremiah, quite simply, hears God speak of his "inner parts."[1] This word is very bold and even somewhat shocking. Jeremiah is the first person to hear God to speak this way, and after him nobody dares to mention this subject in the Old Testament, with just one exception. When the exception comes it is only as a question flung out to God, a question that has as its basis what Jeremiah had heard, but that actually casts doubt on it. It invites

1. French, *entrailles*. (Trans.)

God to confirm or to fill out what was said; "Where then is this deep compassion of your inward parts?" The question is thrown at God, who in the event doesn't answer (Isa 63:15). The answer will eventually be given by Jesus, who comes to break the silence on this issue, telling us in what he says about God's inner feelings all that we have been discovering.

If I allow myself to speak about the inner parts of God, if I dare to do so, it really is not to shock you or to offend God, but for the one and only reason that God himself speaks this way. If I dare to speak of God's feelings and his tenderness it is because *he* speaks of them. Without this I just wouldn't; it would mean being a blasphemer or insane. If Jesus had not himself gone further on this issue, I wouldn't be saying what I am.

What Can Be Said about God? _____

It seems necessary here to enlarge the area of discussion and not avoid the underlying question that presents itself. To speak of the inward parts of God is in effect to speak of God in an anthropomorphic way, to describe him with human traits, which for some is quite unacceptable; they view God as the Completely Other, absolutely unknowable, invisible, inaccessible, incomprehensible, inexpressible, infinitely beyond anything we could say of him. "You are a God who hides himself," it is said (Isa 45:15); he is the one who presents himself to Moses saying, "I am who I am" (Exod 3:14), which comes to the same thing as saying that no one can know him.

All that is so and should never be lost from view; nevertheless, what is to be done when he who hides himself, reveals himself? When the unknowable makes himself known? When the invisible takes human form and allows us to behold his glory? When the inaccessible takes up residence among us? When the incomprehensible enables our hearts to understand? When the Completely Other makes himself

Completely Near and so similar to us? And when the inexpressible gives us the words to speak?

There is no need to renounce a theology of God, the Completely Other, in order to adopt another, that of God the Completely Near; we need to hold the two together because both are true, but they must be held together in the tension of paradox; it is this paradoxical discourse that leads us closer to the truth, which itself is found beyond paradox in the inexpressible.

True, the theology of the Completely Other is correct, but not to look beyond it is to fall into deism, and deism has no need of the Bible to speak of God. A deistic theology is built entirely on human reason, with the knowledge it can have of God without taking into account anything of what God says about himself. Human reason on its own is well able to elaborate a structure in which God is the Completely Other. But human reason is always caught totally off-guard by the biblical revelation, in which God is revealed paradoxically as at one and the same time Completely Other and Completely Near.

What is to be done with a God who opens himself so humbly under human traits and terms, other than to humbly accept ourselves totally wrong-footed in our way of speaking of him? Truly this is disconcerting, but tell me, reader friend, who should teach us to speak of God apart from God himself? So here we find God revealing himself to us as having inward parts, which is to say emotions, and indeed tenderness, in which he even suffers.

If it offends God to speak of him in human terms, would it not also be an offence not to accept what he reveals of himself in human terms, terms as human as the word "inward parts/guts"? To accept the anthropomorphisms proposed by God himself is not blasphemous, insane, out of place, trivial, or indecent; it is to respect him in what he says of himself, and leads us on to understand what there is of the completely other in the anthropomorphisms, to understand that in the inward parts of God there is his inexpressible tenderness.

For a healthy Christian theology such as I am outlining, I believe there are two dangers to avoid; on one hand, to erase from the biblical revelation anything our reason finds unacceptable, anything that does not correspond to our deistic conception of God; on the other, to overcharge the biblical revelation with our imaginings and fantasies. To avoid these two dangers we need to turn ceaselessly back to the Bible to purify our thinking, firstly from inventions of an imagination addicted to anthropomorphisms, and secondly from doubts that arise through God revealing himself in such human terms.

God Confides

"I am moved inwardly." Here God reveals to us that he is deeply moved, inwardly. It is God himself who, on one hand, unveils his tenderness to Jeremiah while on the other he modestly hides it from Ephraim. It is he who hides from one and unveils to the other, as it seems best to him. We need simply to take this in and be silent, as was Jeremiah before such a great mystery. Jeremiah is silent before something God had never previously revealed in such terms. God veils and unveils at one and the same time in a great mystery, a mystery that we see incarnated in Jesus Christ, the mystery that was hidden since before the foundation of the world and unveiled in the fullness of time, he who was the tenderness of God incarnated. Should we be silent before such a mystery, or attempt to speak of it in our stammering human words? It is difficult to know which is the correct position to adopt. Jeremiah also had this concern, was confronted with this dilemma when faced with the content of this oracle. Happily for us he put it in writing and left it for us to encounter, for our meditation, contemplation, wonderment, and thanksgiving.

"I am deeply inwardly moved," says God. Speaking in this very human way, God makes a sort of report on what is going inside him, as if to ask, with a desire to understand, "How is it that I am so moved?"

It is a little foolish to say this of God to be sure, since God knows better than us what we have trouble understanding and knows better than us what it is we don't know. It is not for himself that God speaks in this way, but for us, to help us understand what he experiences; it is a blessing for us to hear God express himself this way. It helps us to better understand the tenderness of God, where it comes from and what triggers it. At the same time it may help us understand ourselves in what we experience.

Behind the Emotion

So what is it here that triggers God's emotions? God tells us himself, it is something he says of Ephraim. "The more I speak of him"—he speaks these words, which awaken the memory he has of him—"the more mindful I am of him." After saying this, God himself draws the conclusion, "this is why I am deeply moved." The words he pronounces and the awakened memory he has of Ephraim point to the bond God has with Ephraim, which causes him to ask himself, "What is Ephraim to me? What is the bond that ties me to him?" The question becomes more specific, "Is he for me a cherished son that I should be so moved? Is he a child in whom I delight, that I should react this way?" Saying this, God pronounces some very strong words in the form of questions, but the implicit answer to the questions is clear and comes across as evidence of what is in his heart; "Yes, that is just what he is to me; a cherished son, a child in whom I delight." Also implicitly, God reveals himself here as a Father and even as maternal Father, which clarifies for us the final statement that so moves him, "I will show him all my tenderness." This is a wonderful interior journey into the depths of the love of God, into the tenderness of a maternal Father.

What Is Left Unsaid

This interior monologue is not directly addressed to Jeremiah. God does not speak directly to his prophet as he did with Ezekiel; there is no "you" in God's mouth. God does, however, speak out loud in the presence of Jeremiah, who he takes as witness, even confidant, since comments of this nature could only be made to someone who is a confidant, or even an intimate.

God does not speak directly to Jeremiah, but is little short of so doing. What he confides has something very fine in that it contains, in particular, an unfinished phrase that reveals again how God's sensitivity is always present. "The more I speak of him," God says, without finishing the sentence. Sure, he "speaks of him," but who to? No doubt it is lovely to speak of Ephraim, but this supposes a listener. To whom does God speak of his cherished son?

The phrase is left hanging; God leaves the listener unnamed, as if veiled, and I believe that the veil is that of delicacy. One does not speak of a cherished son to just anyone. You don't speak to just anyone of the tenderness you feel towards a child you delight in. To whom then is God speaking? It might well be that he is speaking to himself and continuing in this way in profound interior monologue; "the more I speak of him . . . to myself." It could also be that he is speaking to the person who is listening, but out of delicacy not naming the one he is opening his heart to; "the more I speak of him . . . to you, Jeremiah."

However, let us not trouble God in his modesty and let us not specify for someone a place that is not stated anywhere in the oracle. We will leave the text in that indefiniteness that allows us to retain both, perhaps inseparable, meanings; the more I speak of him to myself . . . the more I speak of him to you . . . the more I speak of him to myself in your presence . . . What a delicate intimacy between God and his confidant!

Out loud

God not only speaks of Ephraim, but he is not content to do so just within his own heart; he does so in a way that can be heard by Jeremiah; he speaks out loud. The very fact of speaking of someone out loud can be a source of high emotion. I became very aware of this one day when the father of a family came to me to propose I read a letter he had written to his son, a letter full of love for him, a letter so important that the father wanted to check with me that the terms he used were appropriate and that they conformed to what he wanted to say. When he handed me the letter to read, I asked him if he would read it rather than me. I didn't know what I was unleashing. The father set about reading to me his own letter, to read aloud something he had previously only put in writing. Then, amazingly, when he had scarcely even begun to read, he was overcome by his own emotions, which suddenly took hold of him. He stopped, his eyes full of tears, moved as he was to hear in his own voice the tenderness he felt for his son. Such is tenderness; it moves the one who is full of it even more when it breaks its silence and speaks out loud. It is the same with God.

The Original Source

Looking still more closely at what provokes emotion, we discover in this oracle that the trigger to emotion has itself a trigger. What, so to speak, triggers the trigger of emotion? The oracle is again most instructive on this point.

Why in the first place does God start to talk about Ephraim? What gives birth to his interior monologue? God tells us himself at the start of the oracle—"I can hear Ephraim lamenting." If God starts talking to himself about Ephraim it is because he heard him. It is the fact of hearing him that triggers the monologue; but we need to be more precise.

What God hears is very specific, not just anything, but a complaint, a lamentation, which is to say an expression of pain. Here is the trigger that first causes God's emotion, the suffering of someone else; not some anonymous suffering, but that of Ephraim, his cherished child. It's clear that the tenderness is awoken by the pain of a loved one because the bond of love is touched, perturbed, and wounded. The suffering of a child hits the guts of a father or mother; and such is God deeply moved because one of his children suffers. God is revealed here in all he is as a maternal Father.

We saw the same with regard to little Jerusalem, except that God had not heard the child, but only saw her. Here, God doesn't see Ephraim, he hears him, but in the end it's much the same; God realizes the suffering of a child, whether by seeing or hearing, but one way of the other it is the perception of suffering that so moves him, the suffering of all his cherished children, us among them, reader friend, both you and me, indeed every one of his people.

Like Jerusalem, Ephraim is not one person in particular but a group of people, to be precise, a tribe. In the time of Jeremiah the tribe of Ephraim was not far from being all that remained of the people of God. In the case of Jerusalem, we were concerned with pagans, but with Ephraim, God's chosen. Each, as much as the other, moves God by their sufferings; for every suffering person on earth, God tingles with emotion.

The difference between the suffering of little Jerusalem and the suffering of Ephraim is also that one concerns innocent suffering while the other concerns guilty suffering. The lament of Ephraim is really a confession of someone seized with awareness of his faults, "the shame of his youth," as he says; not shamefulness of which he is a victim, but of which he is the author.

God is deeply moved, as much by innocent as by guilty suffering; he reacts to both, whether in compassionate tenderness or merciful tenderness, and it is on the difference between these two types of tenderness I would like now to pause.

Compassion _____

Etymologically, "compassion" means "suffering with"; this is correct, but we need to be careful because it doesn't mean sharing the suffering of another, to make the suffering of another yours, to suffer in the same way as they do. That is not compassion.

A compassionate person suffers with another, to be sure, but with a different pain than theirs. When a child grazes its knee the compassionate mother does not have a bad knee; the pain is elsewhere, not in the knee, but is inward. If a child is hit on the head, it's the same; the mother doesn't hurt in the head but hurts inwardly.

We see that compassion does not identify itself with the suffering person; it feels badly because of the other, but not in the same way. The suffering of one triggers that of the other, but this latter is inward, which, it seems to me, shows clearly that compassion is nothing other than the suffering of tenderness. Moved inwardly, the compassionate person suffers in his or her tenderness, in the feeling of tenderness towards another.

What does a suffering person look for by turning to someone compassionate? They come looking for tenderness; they have a thirst for this tenderness when in pain, knowing that they will find in tenderness a remedy for their pain, a balm for their wounds. If a hurt child turns towards its mother, it is because he knows, consciously or not, that he will find in her tenderness a comfort that will ease his pain.

I will take the liberty here of telling a story from my childhood that, even though I only understood much later, made this clear. I was about six or seven at the time; the lad who lived in the house next door, a little younger than me, hurt his knee. It was nothing serious, just a graze, but for him, as for me, it was terrible. I was thoroughly disconcerted by the abundance of tears and crying of the boy as he called for his mother, and he seemed paralyzed by his pain. You can imagine the scene! I ran to his house to alert his mother to the terrible situation and urge her to come quickly. I suggested she might like to bring sticking-plaster and iodine thinking these were the appropriate indications. But guess what? The mother told me she had something better than plasters and iodine. She took nothing, but knelt down with her child and delicately kissed his knee. A miracle! The tears and the crying stopped immediately . . . I can tell you that on that day I discovered how tenderness is a very real balm.

Mercy

Mercy is quite different, as we see in the oracle concerning Ephraim. Ephraim is in pain, but not innocently. He is suffering because he has grieved God, and he comes to seek pardon and healing from the very one he has grieved. There is something here that is very different from compassion. In compassion, the sufferer has done nothing to wound or hurt. The lad of whom I spoke had not hurt his mother, and when he was looking to be comforted by motherly tenderness it was simply given to him. On the other hand, when Ephraim comes to seek comfort from the one he has grieved, it is not given so simply. In fact, the merciful person who forgives and comforts a penitent who comes to him, has to draw the forgiveness out of an already hurt tenderness, and, to be more precise, tenderness hurt by the very offence of the person now seeking pardon. This requires of the mercy-giver an overflow of strength. He must first of all overcome the pain of his wounded tenderness, and then give pardon and consolation to the penitent. This shows, I think, the extent to which, for mercy, a greater degree of love is needed than for compassion.

God is a merciful God, to our great joy, but don't forget that the pardon he gives us is drawn out of his aggrieved tenderness, and more precisely from his tenderness grieved by nothing other than our own selves. However, he doesn't show his pain, in his great joy at finding his child. Isn't this what the Parable of the Prodigal Son shows us? The father sheds tears of joy on his son's shoulder, but how many sad tears had he shed previously, before this moment of reunion?

Ephraim's Repentance

Let us spend some time now on Ephraim's repentance, this repentance spoken in the pain of compunction. Look at the repentant words spoken by this cherished son, which God reports as spoken to him. "Cause me to return and I shall return . . . I repent . . . I am ashamed and confused," says Ephraim. It really is God these words are spoken to; this is a real prayer.

The prayer of repentance is magnificent; we find in it all the usual terms found in the mouth of a penitent and there is no doubt that this is not a prayer uttered lightly but from the bottom of the heart. God would not be as moved as he is by a hypocritical prayer. This is a sincere and deep repentance, spoken with such humility that Ephraim even confesses to God his need of strength if he is to fully accomplish it. "Cause me to return and I shall return!" which is as much as to say, "I have need of you if I am to return!" This is so true, but it needs to be said again. Nobody has the hauteur, the audacity, to present himself before God; we just don't have it in us to draw near to him and face up to the grief we have inflicted upon him. The shame and confusion are so great as to cause us to recoil rather than press forward. Who can give a penitent the necessary strength to approach God? Nobody, except for God himself! It is very fine in Ephraim that he humbly asks God for this strength; "Cause me to return and I shall return!"

An Understated Confession

It is a wonderful repentance, but perhaps a little surprising at a first reading because although Ephraim recognizes his fault, "the shame of his youth" as he calls it, it is without ever saying just what the fault was; he doesn't name it. It is a strange repentance which confesses a fault it keeps secret. How can he ask for forgiveness? What exactly is the content of this repentance?

Ephraim doesn't go into the details of his failings, no doubt because he is ashamed, deeply ashamed, as he says himself, "I am ashamed and confused!" Shame, when it is both great and has good reason, inhibits speech to the point of not being able to say certain words. Where modesty causes restraint in the expression of love, shame causes restraint in the expression of guilt!

After all, though, this is not so serious, because God is well aware of the failings in question. He has known Ephraim from his youth and knows all about his disgrace. Perhaps there is even an indication of delicacy on Ephraim's part as he stops himself from further twisting the knife in God's wound. Doesn't David do something quite similar in his great prayer of repentance (Ps 51)? The context of the psalm tells us that he is confessing adultery and murder (51:1), but the prayer in itself does not name the faults confessed.

Indeed, there is something very subtle and admirable here in Ephraim speaking without saying in what his fault consists; he says it in veiled words so as not to grieve God further, but he does, nevertheless, have the courage to say it, despite everything. It is in fact put so discreetly that while God may understand, I suppose that you, the reader, will not have known what the problem is. So what is the fault barely perceptible to our understanding but certainly confessed to God? It was a real disgrace, a failing so serious that Ephraim's reticence is easily understood; it had caused God great grief.

Forgive me then, but no doubt I must now clarify by recalling what Ephraim's youth had been and exactly what the disgrace was to which he alludes.

Ephraim's Disgrace

In Ephraim's confession we find an image, one alone, an image far from flattering, that Ephraim applies to himself, humbly recognizing that it describes him well; "I am like a bullock." This is an image that is no doubt somewhat odd to our taste, but which, in the history of Ephraim, is loaded with meaning. In fact, this image which he now humbly applies to himself, he had first of all outrageously applied to God! Rather than a literary image, Ephraim had made an actual statue; he had made a golden calf, which was erected on a mountain in his territory, and proclaimed to the world that this golden calf was God (1 Kgs 12:28–33), a totally blasphemous insult.

It would be one thing if some accursed pagan had done this, but the calf was made by a cherished son of God, a descendant of Abraham, one who had received all the blessings of the patriarchs. A child in whom God delighted had been so base as to form this statue, which he had installed on mount Ephraim and proclaimed to all the people, "Here is your God, O Israel!" He had even established a clergy with priests to offer sacrifices to the calf.

I have taken the trouble of detailing this as you may not have been aware of it, but you see that Ephraim himself doesn't specify anything because he, like God, has it engraved on his memory; in him, it is a disgrace which he now confesses, carefully stating that the real calf is none other than himself; and in God's memory, it is a deep wound, a wound to his tender affection for his beloved son.

"Like a calf." The word is charged with history and pain. Ephraim says nothing more so as not to grieve God further. Wisely he is careful to invert the picture; the real calf is none other than me!

Not only was the calf an offence towards God, but we are dealing with something that was an offence to his brothers, as Jeremiah knew all too well as a member of the group injured by it. The statue had been made and then raised in a temple by king Jeroboam, the Ephraimite, with the purpose of making visible and formalizing the schism with the tribes of the south and with the tribe of Benjamin in particular. The calf was made to prevent the Ephraimites from going up to the temple in Jerusalem, in the territory of Benjamin; it gives expression to the hunger of the tribe of Ephraim for political and religious hegemony. All of this, Jeremiah, a Benjaminite, knew full well, and could not but hear with sorrow the evocation of the political and religious schism implicit in the mention of the calf.

God is not only grieved by the statue that was made of him, but also to have seen his cherished son separate himself from his brothers, this son for whom he feels such tenderness.

The Grief Caused by the Calf

Wounded tenderness; God suffers this as deeply as one could. Can we measure the full extent of the grief caused to God by the making of the calf? Certainly not. This touches on the unfathomable depths of God; God himself says nothing. The one thing he does that relates to this is found in Hosea 8:5–6, where we hear only his anger, with a promise to crush the calf to pieces. What kind of wound does this anger hide? God keeps this veiled in his modest reserve; when tenderness is so deeply hurt, it maintains silence.

If we know nothing of God's pain as provoked by this calf, we can refer to the other story of a calf, going back to the wilderness, to the time of Moses and Aaron (Exod 32). We can refer to this because, in this very similar offence inflicted on God, the pain of God is a little more perceptible to us, only a little more, but enough to understand what it might have been when Ephraim renewed the offence.

When the first calf was fashioned by Aaron in the wilderness, God and Moses were secluded in conference on Sinai. Moses knew nothing of Aaron's initiative; it is God who informs him of it, spelling out that the calf was meant to represent him—him, the God of Israel! What an offence! As he tells Moses about it, God does not allow his grief to appear; but then suddenly he interrupts the interview, saying simply, "Now let me alone!" (32:10). It is then that Moses understands; these few words are enough for him to realize that God is grieved. The text at this point becomes as terse as it is succinct; "Moses besought (consoled) the face of the Lord" (v. 11). This is a wonderful reaction, that of an intimate who sees his friend grieved; he has understood the grief from the simple words requesting privacy, "Now, let me alone."

God wounded! Oh yes. But the depth of the divine wounding remains beyond the reach of humanity, even to God's friend.

The Imprints of the Wound

True, Moses consoles God in his pain, but the wound has nevertheless left its imprint on God's heart, and of this Moses was in no doubt, as we confirm in the following chapter of Exodus, which reports the ensuing encounter between Moses and God.

In this new meeting, God demonstrates to Moses the extent of his friendship, saying to him, "I will do whatever you ask me, because you have found grace in my eyes" (33:17). To this divine invitation, Moses replies, "Let me see your glory," which is to say, as we find from what follows, "Let me see the glory of your face." Moses without doubt asked too much, because he hears, "You cannot see my face, because no man can see my face and live." However, in order not to go back on the invitation made to his friend, God proposes, "When my glory passes by, I will place you in the cleft of a rock with my hand upon you as I go by. When I withdraw my hand you will see my back, but my face you may not see." And that is what happened.

But tell me, my reader friend, what is the difference between seeing the face of God and dying, and seeing his back and not dying? That is what springs from this passage; had Moses seen God's face, he would have died, and when he saw his back, he didn't die. What is it particularly about the face of God that a human cannot see without dying? The text doesn't give any explanation, but this is what I would propose, and you will do with it, I suppose, as seems good to you.

If God allowed Moses to see his back and not his face, and this so soon after the problem of the golden calf, might it not be because his face still bore traces of his interior grief, signs that could not be seen from behind? What are the signs that a wound to the heart can leave upon a face? The text is silent on this question, but the silence is very significant; might one not think in terms of tears? Forgive me, but it seems to me that God did not want Moses to see his tears! It is very difficult to allow someone else see your tears. In the Orient, as with us, modesty requires a man not to show his tears; would this sensitivity be any less in God than in a human? Here is what, perhaps, underlies God's refusal—"If you were to see my face, Moses, you would see my tears, and you would be overcome by emotion to the point of death! You would be unable to bear to see before your eyes the signs of my grief. That golden calf pains me so much!"

This is certainly true; who could bear to see God's tears?

God's Tears _____

If I am so bold as to bring this out, reader friend, it is really not just some gratuitous hypothesis. It is simply because one day, just the one, it is true, but that is enough, one day with one of his close friends, God soberly and distinctly speaks of his tears. He didn't allow them to be seen of course, any more that he did with Moses, but he does speak of them. This intimate friend of God you already know because it is Jeremiah, him again! Here is what God said to him as a word to be communicated, no doubt to touch peoples' hearts and enable them better to know God: "You will say to them the following—'tears stream down from my eyes day and night and never cease, because my daughter, this young virgin, has been dealt a heavy blow'" (14:17). It is a Father who speaks here, weeping over the suffering of his daughter. The daughter in question is none other than Jerusalem again, his well-beloved.

Such is God! Such is our God, reader friend! A Father capable of weeping with affection over his children, he loves them so much. No one has seen his tears; but the Son sheds them over Jerusalem.

There we have everything, it seems to me, that lies behind this story of the calf, everything of which Ephraim was ashamed to speak, everything that plunges him into the pain of compunction; we see his repentance as a cherished son returning to a divine father he has so deeply wounded, and how this repentance moves God to the depths of his being. Here is this Father so moved that he cannot bring himself to speak directly to his darling son but turns to Jeremiah, his confidant, and opens to him his heart.

The Love That Moves God

All this being so, we understand that Ephraim both wishes to renew the relationship with God by asking forgiveness, and is full of hesitation about approaching him since his shame holds him back so much. "Cause me to return and I will return!"

But this is not all. There is also in what Ephraim says another statement, another reality that could not but touch God's love deeply, and move him to the utmost degree.

As we have seen, Ephraim is sufficiently delicate not to go into any detail that might twist the knife in God's wound; and it is also with much delicacy that he drops into God's heart the following words, which reveal the attachment he has for him—"You are the Lord, my God." Not simply, "You are the Lord God," but "You are the Lord, *my* God," with this discreet but no less superb "my," which is enough to touch God to the highest degree because it expresses a true bond of love. After the story of the golden calf, this discreet confession of love is enough to move God to the core and mollify his wound. "If I am

God to him, even his God, what then is he for me? Is he a cherished son, a child in whom I delight?"

Repentance That Consoles

This is still not all. I believe that something else that touches God deeply is another word from Ephraim's confession, a word whose force cannot be conveyed by our translation—"I repent." The Hebrew word *nākham* used by Ephraim has a double meaning because it signifies both to repent and to console, which is impossible to translate.

What is the link between the two meanings of the word, between repenting and consoling? I think it is easy to understand, even if it takes a little time. A person who repents and goes to seek forgiveness of the one he has hurt may not always be aware of it but in fact he does console. Undoubtedly you will have experienced in your life the truth of this; when someone comes to ask forgiveness of you they do bring solace for the wrong done.

That is what is going on here. "I repent," says Ephraim, and in saying it he consoles God. This is indeed what God feels when he hears this in the mouth of his cherished son; this is why he is moved to the core, to his paternal core. His beloved son who has grieved him comes himself to console him by asking of him forgiveness.

Repentance is a balm to God's pain, to his wounded tenderness.

You know, reader friend, since the day I understood this about repentance and learned that in asking pardon of God I was bringing him comfort for the wrong I had done him and the wounds I had caused him, then for me repentance became instinct with a certain joy; it is certainly no longer a sort of quaint exercise, a pious obligation, a formality. I know that it humbly brings to God a balm that does him good; it manages to touch the untouchable in his grieving tenderness and quietens it. This is a deep mystery; a blessed mystery . . . !

Yes, God is indeed the Completely Other, infinitely other than we can think of him, and yet he reveals himself as Completely Near, so close in fact that we can console him.

Active Tenderness

"I will show him all my tenderness." The translation is again a bit feeble. In fact, the expression is unique in this form in the Old Testament. There is a double reinforcement of the word, which in Hebrew is an expression of the absolute superlative, as if of a sort of super-tenderness, a tenderness still more sweet, strong, deep, and overwhelming than every other tenderness put together. We understand that, after expressing himself like this, God is so moved that he is unable to continue speaking and becomes silent; there has never been a silence pregnant with such great tenderness.

"To show tenderness." The Hebrew verb is not a verb of state but of action. It does not describe a state of tenderness in which one finds oneself, but what the tenderness is impelled to *do* in favor of its recipient; this is the tenderness of God—it is active! It relieves, pardons, rehabilitates, reconciles, restores, heals, brings peace. . . . When the father of the prodigal falls on the neck of his son he is full of active tenderness. But this doesn't change the fact that the signs of the tenderness might remain entirely hidden behind the veil of modesty; Jesus, in an overflow of tenderness, finds himself impelled by it to revive the son of the widow at Nain, but confines all the force of his tenderness to the intonation of his voice as he says, "Don't cry."

How is God going to show Ephraim his tenderness? By forgiving as Ephraim asks. Forgiveness, the fruit of merciful tenderness, is in God's case alone an extremely active reality; it is a very real work that accomplishes things; forgiveness frees the other from his fault, heals him from sorrow or from anguish, and gives him new life.

"I am going to show him all my tenderness." Another point to mention about the Hebrew expression is that the verb used describes the present situation but has a tense form that looks to the future. Though tenderness impels God to forgive, there may be a certain delay before the manifestation of the forgiveness. Is God so moved that he needs some time to get over his feelings and speak his pardon? I don't believe so—it is something else.

Time to Receive Forgiveness

If God does not immediately express his forgiveness it is because he knows that Ephraim will need some time to prepare himself to receive it.

We often go too quickly in asking forgiveness, too quickly in giving it, too quickly in each stage, which means that it is often very superficial. Time is needed for repentance to be spoken from the bottom of the heart; time is needed if the pardon given is to be drawn from deep down. As we have seen, the one who pardons needs to take his time to get past the pain of his wound, to lift the sadness of the wound and transform it into the joy of forgiveness. This, of course, does not require time on God's part, but so far as Ephraim is concerned, a period of time is necessary, time to open himself to God's forgiveness.

All of this appears very clearly in the account of the woman taken in adultery (John 8). Jesus takes his time to tell the woman that she is forgiven. He takes this time not because he is not ready to give it, but because she is not ready to hear it. As the situation stands, the woman's heart is closed because of the kangaroo court gathered around her; and with her heart closed she would not be able to hear. Jesus gives the woman the time she needs to open up and does what is necessary to enable this. He sets himself to writing on the ground and takes his time over it; he also humbly puts himself in a position lower than her and not in the attitude of a judge. Then he speaks to the people around her in such a way that they all withdraw and Jesus is then alone with the woman. She thus discovers, little by little, that the "court" has disappeared, and that Jesus is not a judge. This time allows her to make an internal journey, to adjust, to open her heart little by little, and finally receive the word of forgiveness.

How does God propose to show his forgiveness to Ephraim? I think it is easy to see; it is enough just to read the neighboring oracles and all becomes clear. God's forgiveness will be manifest in return from exile.

"Cause Me to Return"

When Jeremiah receives the oracle concerning Ephraim, this tribe, like all the northern tribes, had been in exile for decades. The lament God hears is spoken in exile, which invites us to understand it in two ways. Firstly it means what we have already understood—"Cause me to turn to you in repentance and I will return"; but it also means, "Cause me to return *from exile* and I will return." God understands it all; he hears the repentance of the exiled people and it moves him to the core. He responds by according them both pardon and return from exile. Return from exile will be the manifestation, the concrete and visible proof, of his pardon.

Why wait and not bring Ephraim back without further delay? To allow Ephraim time to understand one thing, that God has heard his prayer, not as coming from Jerusalem, but from the land of his exile, because God himself left and went with Ephraim into exile! He is to be found right at their side in a distant land. God is there with him, at his side, at the side of his beloved son in whom he delights. God is waiting for Ephraim to open his heart to the reality of his divine presence. The Completely Other is the Completely Near, and to assimilate this takes time. It takes so long to realize the degree to which God is near. The oracles that announce the return from exile don't say, "I am going to come and look for my people in exile," but use words that mean that God is already with them, among them; "because I am with you to deliver you" (Jer 30:11); "I am now bringing back the exiles from the land of the north" (31:8); "I will lead them in the midst of their supplications, and will bring them by a pathway on which they will not falter" (31:9).

The Mercy of God Precedes Our Repentance

I also believe we should note the way all the oracles about the return from exile are not found after but before the short oracle we are considering. The return is not announced *after* Ephraim's lament but before it. God's mercy is not asleep, as if waiting to be awoken by our prayer; his mercy precedes our prayer. In his tenderness, God is already at our side before we even ask him. The prodigal son was already in the merciful arms of his father when he asked for pardon; he had already perceived the good, happy tears of his father before he ever pronounced the first words of his repentance. Moreover, this wonderful father had already prepared the robe, the ring, and the sandals for his son, expecting his return. Everything was ready for the feast! In the same way, the promises of God had already been delivered to Jeremiah, already lodged in the heart of his confidant, before ever Ephraim had taken the first step of repentance. Divine tenderness magnificently precedes us and mysteriously envelops us before we even begin to perceive it; it is already secretly at work in our hearts preparing and opening us to its mystery.

The Tenderness of Forgiveness

God's forgiveness is always given in tenderness; it is woven into it, impregnated with it. There is no exception to this and I don't believe it could be otherwise because God is all love, all tenderness. We have already noted how mercy without tenderness is mercy that works ill, and this is not the case with God. While our mercy may become condescending, without love, and perhaps with a touch of disdain that wounds the one seeking pardon, there is nothing in that of God; he, in truth, is just the same with everyone as he is here with Ephraim.

The tenderness of God's pardon is, nevertheless, not always felt, because, as you know, it comes veiled in divine delicacy. But there is another reason that makes it difficult or even impossible to feel this tenderness. This reason has nothing to do with God and his modesty, but with us, or more exactly with our heart, which is not always ready to recognize God's tenderness. Our eyes don't always see the signs of his tenderness, our ears do not always hear his words of tenderness or the tone of his voice because our heart is not so disposed as to understand the merciful tenderness that accompanies God's forgiveness.

Here is a biblical example that seems to me to clarify the point. It concerns the healing of the paralytic at Capernaum whose four friends lowered him to the feet of Jesus. The healing is reported by each of the first three Gospels, but we should note that the three of them are not equally sensitive to the tenderness Jesus shows the paralytic at the moment when he indeed announces the forgiveness of his sins. "Your sins are forgiven," he tells him; but the three evangelists report these words of Jesus in different ways.

Matthew and Mark did observe the tenderness of Jesus. They report what he said in its entirety; that is, including the vocative that introduces it: "My child, my son, your sins are forgiven" (Matt 9:2; Mark 2:5). In this "my child" there is a real tenderness if we consider the Greek word used (*teknon*), which is regarded by all the Greek dictionaries as a term of affection. This is the only time that Jesus speaks to a man, an adult, in this way, a man he had never seen before and who he had never heard speak. If Jesus speaks like this to the suffering paralytic it is because he is inwardly moved towards him, moved with tenderness: "my child!"

98

"Your sins are forgiven," Jesus says, making himself the bearer of God's forgiveness, as was well understood by the witnesses of the scene, who are offended and cry out that it was blasphemy, since only God forgives. In fact, Jesus not only makes himself the bearer of God's pardon but also of the tenderness tied to the pardon. "My child, your sins are forgiven." Christ here reveals the Father, to the extent of presenting himself as having the heart of a father—"my child."

That's how Matthew and Mark perceived the tenderness with which Jesus gives forgiveness, not giving lightly but from deep inward mercy.

The Heart Does Not Always Perceive

In Luke it is rather different; here he is not at all sensitive to Jesus' tenderness towards the paralytic. In other places Luke is very attentive to Jesus' tenderness, as we saw in the account of the widow of Nain, which he alone records; he is also alone in recording the extraordinary Parables of the Good Samaritan and the Prodigal Son. But what we find from his pen here is not, "my child your sins are forgiven you," but, "man, your sins are forgiven you" (5:20). What a difference between "my child" and "man"! The second word has no tenderness in it; it is even distant, abrupt. The account is otherwise the same; the tenderness of Jesus has simply escaped one evangelist but not the others.

How is it that the heart is not always disposed to perceive the tenderness that is as constant in the Son of God as in his Father? I am not saying this of Luke, who is elsewhere wonderfully perceptive, but of us, who are more often incapable. How is it that the heart of man perceives so poorly or not at all the tenderness of God when it was made to do so? Quite simply it is because the heart of man is hard, too hard to notice something so tender. The hard heart is about as sensitive as a rock.

Hardness of heart; this is an immense subject to open. The Bible has plenty to say about it because God himself is the first person confronted by and exposed to our hardness of heart. He acts towards us with infinite tenderness but he also finds himself the object of the hardness of our heart, as you know as well as me, unfortunately.

What is it that so hardens the heart? Well, quite simply it is our sin, which shuts us off from God, from his love and from his tenderness. It is our obstinate resistance to everything that comes from him, which is what the church fathers referred to as our spiritual sicknesses, our passions. For the fathers, occasional sin was not so serious, because it is not enough to harden the heart; what is serious is sin that is repeated, that installs itself and becomes habitual and chronic—this is a spiritual sickness; this is what hardens the heart, so deeply that the sickness digs itself in over time. Resentment hardens the heart; avarice hardens the heart, hatred too . . . All the spiritual sicknesses, at the end of the day, harden the heart little by little, absolutely all of them, as is affirmed by the fathers, who were so very concerned about this important aspect of our spiritual life; it is so important because at stake is our love relationship with God, our sensitivity to his tenderness.

We need to realize that these sicknesses, which are expressed and appear in our actions, in our behavior, are already present in our thoughts, which can be literally contaminated. Before they lead to actions, evil thoughts live in our heart and make it hard. We need, then, to examine our thoughts, to see if any spiritual sickness is evident there; and also look at the state of our heart and its hardness and insensitivity to the tenderness of God, to the gentleness of his tenderness.

The sensitivity, delicacy, and modesty of God on one hand, and the hardness of our heart on the other: this is the combination that makes it difficult or impossible for us to perceive the tenderness of God. If we want things to change, we need to roll up our sleeves and attack, not of course God's modesty, but, with God's merciful help, those things that make our hearts so hard.

The Pitiless Servant _____

God's modesty and our hardness of heart; these two realities are beautifully exemplified in a parable of Jesus that I am content to mention briefly here and leave to your further meditation. This is the Parable of the Pitiless or Unforgiving Servant, which is reported only by Matthew (18:21–35); Jesus puts it forward in response precisely to a question about forgiveness.

The parable introduces us to a king, but we know that by this king Jesus wishes to speak of his Father, without however naming him, so as to operate by suggestion. He only lifts the veil in the final verse. What passes between the king and his servants speaks of what passes between God and ourselves.

You know the parable; the king wishes to settle accounts with his servants, and one of them owes an astronomical sum that he cannot possibly pay back. The servant throws himself on the ground before the king and begs him for time to settle up. It is a foolish request, but it touches the king who, Jesus specifies, was "moved to the core" (v. 27).

We then see the king so deeply moved that he goes far beyond the request of his servant and remits the entire debt. It is total forgiveness and absolute mercy, and all within the infinite tenderness that permeates divine mercy; nevertheless, because this is a king, the pardon is given and the debt remitted without the slightest apparent trace of tenderness. Protocol demands it; a king does not allow his tenderness to be seen by a simple servant! This expresses the extreme of propriety that God may adopt; he is the King of kings.

There we have God's side, an extremely generous pardon issuing from the depths of his being. What of the servant, who knows himself to have been forgiven but without knowing what has motivated, dictated the forgiveness; who is entirely ignorant of the king's tenderness but nevertheless enjoys its fruit?

You know the rest; the servant calls one of his fellows who owes him a pittance, and in his turn throws himself on the ground to beg for time to pay the servant back. The prayer has absolutely no impact on the heart of the servant, who is pitiless and does not remit the debt. Nothing is said to describe the state of the man's heart, but clearly it is particularly hard. Hardness of heart; this explains why even in the presence of the king he was insensible of the royal mercy, insensitive to his tenderness. Had the king allowed something of his tenderness to be seen, the servant still would not have noticed, his heart was so hard. How poor we are; God could renounce his restraint and openly show his tenderness, but it would be in vain because with our hardness of heart it would still be beyond our grasp.

Tenderness Mocked

The violence expressed at the end of the parable also demands our attention. "The angry lord handed his servant over to the torturers." How can this king, capable of being moved so deeply on behalf of his servant, now react with such violence to the servant who shows himself so unforgiving? Is God like that? No doubt, as Jesus expressly tells us when he concludes the parable by likening the heavenly Father to this king (v. 35). But I do believe this demands an explanation.

Like every parable this one is a teaching aid. It is told to help us make progress, to put us on the right track to living in God's tenderness, but without being mistaken about it. Once again, the tenderness of God is not weak. It is demanding and doesn't open the door to permissiveness; it is not to be taken lightly, as this would distort it and deprive it of its motivating force. To regard the tenderness lightly is to take away the force of its compassion and mercy. To take seriously the merciful tenderness of the God who forgives, allows us to live by this tenderness and to forgive in turn. Not to take it seriously is not to take God seriously in the profundity of his forgiveness and is indeed to mock God. That, I believe, is the real force of the teaching in this parable.

"The angry lord"—the lord is really furious and he allows the passion that issues from his wounded love to be expressed. We see that the anger of God is the cry of his wounded love. There is nothing to be done when faced with it than to expose ourselves to it humbly with compunction, to throw ourselves down and plead, hoping that the angry king will again be touched by our bitter tears of repentance.

"Lord my God, in your grace and mercy, would you again forgive my attitude which is so grievous to you, so lacking in respect for your tenderness, so unforgiveable even. Would you again have pity on me who hurt you in this unforgiveable way; help me to soften my heart which is so hard and pitiless so that eventually I might correctly honor your tenderness!"

To Soften the Heart

What shall we do with our hard heart? Well, break it, quite simply! There is nothing else to be done with it, and this is repentance; it breaks the heart and we live with a broken heart as the great psalm of repentance says: "A broken and a contrite heart, O God, you will not despise" (51:19). The miracle is that in his unfathomable and tireless mercy, God welcomes and gives his forgiveness to the heart broken by repentance . . . how wonderful!

As we have seen, repentance has its beginning in compunction, in the heart that grieves to have hurt God. What can we now say about this compunction that is the source of repentance and the softening of the heart?

To speak of the breaking of a hard heart is to bring before our eyes something very painful, and that is just what compunction is. As we saw, the Greek word translated as compunction (*katanuxis*) evokes the pain of piercing stabs. The picture is different to that of breaking, but the reality of the suffering is right there, the pain of having grieved God.

What is the internal process that can lead from this heartfelt suffering to the softening of the heart where the heart is able to perceive God's tenderness?

I have mentioned that the word compunction is very rare in the Bible and that the best witness to it is in the book of the Acts of the Apostles. There is nothing else in the New Testament, so that the biblical texts don't help us dig any deeper into the notion. The church fathers lived compunction and became well able to speak of it, not so much by their analysis of biblical texts as by their own experience. Here is what they discovered by experience about compunction and what we can discover as we live it, that is to say, as we live out the repentance that is its inseparable extension.

The Experience of the Fathers

The fathers experienced repentance on a daily basis and teach us to do the same. They were right in this; we grieve God all the time and in a thousand ways, so we should always be repenting in a spirit of compunction.

By living out compunction on a daily basis, the fathers became aware that the pain of compunction gradually lessens, shading little by little into a softness that takes its place. Little by little, compunction changes from painful to gentle, without ceasing to be compunction. This explains why the fathers found it necessary to invent a new word, passing from *katanuxis* to *eukatanuxis*, signifying by the addition of the paradoxical prefix *eu*, which means good, how compunction can mysteriously contain in itself a real gentleness. We could say that the pain of the heart is en route to be transformed into a "tender pain" of the heart, to use a paradoxical phrase.

This is what repentance brings over time. Repentance doesn't simply emerge as a softening of the heart as though we were speaking of two successive stages, as if repentance ceased and became something else. No, repentance, by the grace of God, is so constituted as to contain in itself the softening of the heart and thus should not have an end. It becomes soft and gentle while remaining sorrowful. How do we explain this transformation, the internal transformation of repentance? What causes repentance to carry in itself the softening of the heart?

The fathers draw our attention to the fact that repentance is normally accompanied by tears, whether external or internal tears. The penitent weeps, as we see with Peter the moment he realizes he has denied Christ. "He wept bitterly" (Luke 22:62), and then sorrowfully. Tears of compunction gradually come to soften the heart. But really it is little by little, over the course of years even, like drops of water, finally piercing the heart of stone, a long and slow work that would take an infinity of time if that was all there is to it. Our tears are essential, not to be avoided, but they are not the only factor, happily for us.

Tears, such is our part in a process that softens the heart, but it is actually a very small part compared to the part God plays; his part is fundamental and the fathers dwell on this at much greater length, and rightly so.

The Softening of Tears

The softening of the heart is the work of God, a gift of God; it is not a gift that crowns some merit gained by repentance, but really the gift of his grace, not at the end of our repentance, but as it proceeds, in the midst of it, a progressive gift lasting throughout repentance.

God deposits this gift in our heart during the prayer of repentance, in such a way that the penitent goes along , discovering, little by little, a gentleness like no other because it comes from God. It is sweeter than honey, sweeter than any sweetness.

This sweetness is given in response to our request for forgiveness; it is the sweetness of God's forgiveness. To receive God's forgiveness is to receive intense sweetness, the sweetness of pardon, not just from anybody, but from God himself. More exactly, as God's forgiveness is always given in the tenderness of mercy we can say the sweetness of forgiveness is nothing other than the sweetness of God's tenderness. That's why it is sweetness without equal, the sweetness of the tenderness of God. Do you have hold of this? God comes to touch the heart of the penitent with tenderness and to fill it with sweetness; this sweetness is beyond description. You can understand why little by little the bitter tears of compunction become sweet, that divine sweetness which, deposited into the heart, communicates itself through the entire being of the penitent, into the body and soul. It is a miracle, the pure grace of God.

When the father in the parable welcomes the prodigal, the son is weeping the bitter tears of repentance. But the father, throwing himself into his arms, is so happy to find him that he weeps tears of joy, tears so sweet they transform the tears of the son. The son, as he enters into the joy of his father, also begins to weep tears of great sweetness, the sweetness of knowing himself to be tenderly loved. This blessed embrace unites them in tenderness.

It is thus the sweetness of the father's tenderness that softens the heart of the son. That is just how it is for us; the sweetness of God's tenderness softens our heart. There is an indescribable softness in our heart that flows from the sweetness of the tenderness of God himself.

When the prodigal was far away, his father considered him lost, as if dead (v. 24), and shed bitter tears of sorrow over him. But the bitter tears of the father become sweet when the son appears at the end of the road; the bitter tears of the son become sweet in the arms of his father. The father comforts the prodigal son, and the prodigal son comforts the father. This happy embrace unites them in tenderness.

The sweetness of God's tenderness as it communicates itself to us is such that it brings to birth in us tenderness for him. God does not demand of us tenderness, he communicates it to us. We discover that we are moved to the core of our being as we contemplate this God who humbly accepts being consoled by our repentance.

In the Bible, God commands us to love him with all our heart, with all our soul and with all our strength, but never with all our inward parts to the very bowels, and so with all our tenderness. Never! God never makes the claim on us to be loved with all our tenderness! But wait . . . he brings to birth this tenderness in the embrace of his forgiveness. I am aware, as I read, how some of the church fathers had a real tenderness for God, an astonishing tenderness that they wrap and conceal with more or less of great reserve, to the point of not speaking of it. They are silent, but it can be perceived in the silence because it can still be sensed between the lines. The tenderness of humanity for God is born mysteriously in the mystery of the prayer of repentance; it stems from the tenderness of God towards humanity.

Sweetness and Pain

The softening of the heart through compunction doesn't mean that sadness disappears; it stays, but is being transformed. It stays because the heart, as it grows softer, also becomes more sensitive, and in particular more sensitive to the multiple wounds to which God is subjected from every quarter. The softened heart begins to suffer for God, to feel for his wounds. The pain of compassion for God is therefore added to the pain of compunction. One day, after witnessing with me a harrowing scene in which we were unable to intervene, a parishioner said to me, "How much that must hurt God!" Happy the man whose heart is full of compassion for God.

At the same time, the softened heart begins to suffer for those who wound God, with compassion for them also as it sees how they suffer from the weight of their faults. This compassion for others is also added to compunction. In this way compunction extends to others in just the way Christ alerts us to when he invites us to say to God, not, "Forgive me my offences," but, "Forgive us our offences."

This enlargement subtly blends with compunction the sweetness of a certain tenderness towards others and God.

We Are Also Confidants

The fact that God cloaks his tenderness in great modesty brings to our awareness the most important role of the few intimates to whom God gives the grace of raising a little the veil of this modesty; he does this so that they may contemplate his tenderness a little more closely. I am thinking of those confidants of God we've already spoken about a little and it would be good to talk a little more about them now, remembering that, as witnesses, they are particularly well placed to speak of God's tenderness.

Moses, Jeremiah, and Ezekiel were confidants of God, just as the disciples were confidants of the Son of God, and it is on the disciples that I would like to dwell a little now in order to better understand the place and role of a confidant—on the disciples specifically because we can more easily recognize ourselves in them. In fact, we, as disciples ourselves, are called to fill the place of confidants. This is why we need to really take hold of what the role of a confidant is.

Many passages in the Gospels teach us that Jesus was moved inwardly and that he could also be touched in his tenderness. We have noticed this in the story of his encounter with the widow of Nain; but on other occasions too there is the issue of his being moved in this way. With regard to all these occasions there is one, just one, in which Jesus himself confesses his inward feelings; in each of the others the feeling is signaled by the evangelists, who notice it in one way or another, but without Jesus having said anything. Just one time then Jesus reveals his emotions by saying, "I am moved to the core." Just the one time! This tells us the degree to which he was always very reserved. To which intimate friend did he make this confession? Well, to those who were closest, to his disciples, who therefore appear as his confidants. What was the occasion when Jesus lifted the veil on his sense of modesty?

It happened in a desert place with a crowd that had been without food for three days. Knowing that the hungry people would not have enough strength to get home, Jesus was moved inwardly. The situation of great need moved him; it is then that he gave them something to eat. The situation was the multiplication of bread, to be precise, the second occasion.

"I am moved inwardly" (Matt 15:32; Mark 8:2). Jesus didn't say this to the crowd but to his disciples, although what had moved Jesus was the crowd and not the disciples. We see that the confidants learn something that does not really concern them so much as others who know nothing of the emotion and tenderness from which they are to benefit. Jesus is moved by the crowd and they know nothing of it! The crowd receives the bread without knowing the way the bread is a carrier of tenderness, so great is Jesus' modesty. This is just like the brother asleep on the knees of Abba Poemen, unaware of the modest tenderness of the Abba. What a lesson for us who are so much more the beneficiaries of the tenderness of God without knowing it, his tenderness being so veiled in modesty.

The Role of Confidants

Let us return to the disciples as confidants, perfectly informed and perfectly aware of the tenderness Jesus feels. What is their role to be? Jesus doesn't ask them to go and proclaim his tenderness to the crowd. Modesty is the crucial factor! On the contrary, he just tells them to go and hand out the bread, the bread that results from the tenderness. What a mission; how were they to do it? Were they to distribute this bread of tenderness without speaking of the tenderness? That is certainly what the text seems to suggest. Would they have been able to distribute the bread without revealing the tenderness? Jesus did not brief them either way; it was left to each one to decide what it suited him to say, if anything. The fact is that the disciples bore in their hands the bread of tenderness and in their heart everything they knew about this tenderness. It seems that the disciples said nothing, but I imagine they would not have handed the bread out just any old how. Certainly not like automatons. Everything invites us to think that they must have made an effort, by whatever means, to make known how charged the bread was with tenderness. They had a treasure of tenderness in their hands. The same sense fills my heart when I hand round the bread of Communion.

These are a few reflections on the mission of a confidant, and they should raise, I believe, a constant questioning within ourselves, how to transmit to others the immense tenderness that God has for them? How to unveil it without mishandling the modesty in which it is cloaked?

Why didn't Jesus himself distribute the bread to the crowd? Is it to modestly keep a certain distance and not allow his feelings to show? Is it so as to be sure to have his feelings perfectly under control? I have no idea; but the fact is that he retreats behind his confidants, as God is self-effacing behind Ezekiel when it is time to tell Jerusalem the events of her birth; as he is self-effacing when he tells only Jeremiah how moved he is by Ephraim; as he is self-effacing in the cloud on Sinai when he tells Moses alone, "I am a God of tenderness," in his humble and modest tenderness.

Is it always so? Does he always hide self-effacingly behind his confidants; does he always need them if others are to glimpse his tenderness? Not always, as Jesus helps us understand; the father in the parable had no need of anyone else to enfold his son in his arms . . . !

Apprenticeship

How is a confidant to transmit the divine tenderness he or she has encountered? How were the disciples to convey to the crowd what they knew of the tenderness of Jesus towards them? How did they distribute the bread at the time of the miracle, which is both a miracle of multiplication of bread and a miracle of tenderness unveiled to confidants?

Christ said nothing precise about how to let his tenderness be known; it remains something requiring great discernment on the part of the disciples, and this is a very important point for us. I imagine that, knowing what I do of the tenderness of God, you would be itching with the desire to speak to all the world around you. If that is the case, don't go too fast! Personally I have been quite foolish enough at times! Take time to pray, to ask God to give you the necessary discernment; his tenderness is not to be published in just any way, to just anyone, or under just any circumstance. When should we speak about God's tenderness? When others are ready to listen? When should we speak and when be content with actions? And with what actions should we let it be known? This all requires a real discernment, which God alone can give through prayer. I can give a simple example, but it is not always so easy. It's possible to speak of the tenderness of God to a dying old lady with a caress to her face. On every occasion we should take time to pray and discern what is most suitable to say or not to say, to do or not to do.

Further to this, how are we to transmit to others the tenderness of God if we are not ourselves aware of it? Here again, we just mustn't go too fast. We must take time to allow ourselves to be permeated with the tenderness of God; then we can really witness to it and be bearers of it. I imagine that Paul must have taken this time before he could write to the Philippians, "I long after you all with the tenderness of Jesus Christ" (1:8). He didn't say, "I long after you with my own tenderness," but, "I long after you with the tenderness of Jesus Christ." He must have been full of that tenderness to be able write this way!

There we have it; a confidant who is full of the tenderness of God witnesses to it in word, as also in silence, in conduct, in a look, by this or that action, and also with a real modest delicacy, a delicacy that both veils and unveils the tenderness at the same time; may the Lord help us!

At School with the Confidant *par excellence* _____

Given the extent and complexity of the mission that is the task of a confidant, a question arises rather powerfully; who will teach us to be confidants of God? In whose school should we enroll?

I believe the answer is straightforward; the only teacher to whom we can turn is Christ, the true confidant of the Father. So, let us pause for a while to discover how Christ went about speaking or demonstrating the tenderness of God.

I don't wish to repeat what has already been said, but I will briefly recap in order to renew your meditation and reflection on this point.

Jesus unveils the tenderness of his Father in his teaching, and in particular in the parables like those about the prodigal son and the pitiless servant; we won't go over that again.

As well as by teaching, Jesus shows this tenderness by his conduct in personal encounters, as we have seen, for example, in the "don't weep" he speaks to the widow at Nain, or the "my son, your sins are forgiven you" spoken to the paralytic at Capernaum.

I would like now to take some other examples not mentioned earlier, which directly concern the disciples, considered this time not as witnesses of the tenderness of Jesus but as beneficiaries of the divine tenderness he incarnates.

Jesus is so full of the tenderness of his Father that he speaks to his disciples as the Father would speak. This appears very clearly when he calls them "my children." Speaking this way, Jesus clearly takes the role of a father, and clearly reveals the Father. In each case we will see how the Father he incarnates is full of tenderness.

There are just three passages where Jesus speaks in this way to the disciples, each time with a different word in the Greek. Unfortunately our translations poorly convey the diversity of these words because we are not as rich as the Greeks in this area. We will search these three passages and discover how Jesus reveals the tenderness of God, which he incarnates.

Washing the Feet of His Little Children

The first of the three passages is found in John's Gospel in chapter 13. Jesus speaks to his disciples and calls them, "my little children" (v. 33). Nowhere else does he speak like this to anyone. It is rather surprising to see him address adults, men in their prime, this way—and without at all demeaning them. The Greek word used, *teknia*, is a diminutive of the word Jesus used to address the paralytic, *teknon*. With the paralytic it was a term of affection, and the diminutive is even more affectionate.

What disposed Jesus to adopt such an affectionate tone with his great strapping lads of disciples? Why does he consider them children? I don't see anything in what he actually says to them that gives an answer to these questions. However, the manner of speech is explained by what has just happened; Jesus had washed the feet of his disciples. This act is surely that of a servant, even a slave, which reveals the extreme humility of Jesus, who lowers himself to the rank of servant. This seems obvious and is the first level of interpretation of the scene. However, a servant wouldn't be saying, "my little children," to those whose feet he washes; so there is something else in question. The gesture is also one of a mother who is caring for her children at an age when they are too young to wash their feet for themselves. She could say to them, "my little children." As well as the humility of a servant, we discover here the tenderness of a mother who is full of affection. That, it seems to me, is what is contained in this "my little children" in the mouth of Jesus, who appears here as a true maternal father, embodying the tenderness of God the Father, himself so maternal.

At their age the disciples are quite big enough to wash their own feet, but, as Jesus tells them, they are not able to wash, purify themselves completely. Like them, we have great need of God, who in the tenderness of his love is alone capable of purifying us so that we are entirely pure, right to the core. I believe that in this act of Jesus we can see the tenderness of God the Father, who washes our heart with the same gentleness as if he was washing the feet of a little child.

Feeding the Little Children

In another passage in the same Gospel (21:5), Jesus calls the disciples by a word that is not used to address anyone else, and which is translated again by the phrase, "my little children," but which in the Greek is something else again, *paidia*. This word indicates a child less than seven years old, a really astonishing notion to see applied to the disciples. Once again, what leads Jesus to speak this way? The vocative, "my little children," is accompanied by the following words, "do you have nothing to eat?" Jesus is concerned here about their food, and we learn shortly afterwards that he has prepared for them some grilled fish and bread (v. 9). We discover Christ here once again in the attitude of a mother who has prepared something to eat for her little children, at an age when they are too young to know how to cook fish or bake bread. "My little children," says he who discreetly reveals the tenderness of a maternal Father.

Reassuring the Children _____

The final passage where Jesus addresses his disciples, calling them "my children," here *tekna*, is found in Mark's Gospel (10:24). This is just after the encounter with the rich young man and his departure. The disciples are agog with expectation, amazed by Jesus' comments that "it is difficult for the rich to enter the kingdom the heaven" (v. 23). Jesus continues, "my children, it is more difficult than for a camel to pass through the eye of a needle," which puzzles the disciples even more. It is into this growing astonishment that Jesus slips his "my children," which has no aim other than to reassure them in their fears about their own salvation. Have no fear, my children, because what is impossible with men is possible with God! Be as confident with God as children are with their father.

Something here that shows very nicely that Jesus takes the role of a father for the disciples is seen in discreet detail. In this way, at the end of this account, Jesus defines disciples as those who have left everything. He enumerates, "house, brothers, sisters, mother, father, children, lands." When he continues that the disciples will receive in return one hundredfold, he goes through the same list, but this time there is one omission—the father! What's this? The disciples will not receive back fathers by the hundredfold? No. They already have one father who is worth far more than a hundred! The father in question is none other than the one who calls them "my children"!

Sentimental tenderness reduces the other person to a child, but there is nothing of that in the mouth of Jesus. Never, moreover, has the tenderness of Jesus ever done that to anyone.

Another notable feature of this text is that Jesus' words are accompanied by a look; "he looked at them," the text says (v. 27), using a rare word (*emblepō*) that means exactly "to look deeply," that is, to look deep into the heart. The same word had just been used by Mark to describe the way Jesus had looked fixedly at the rich young man (v. 21), and the word is associated with another which tells us what is conveyed by this look; "he looked at him and loved him." All of Jesus' love for the rich man is in the silent look. The repetition of the word to describe the look Jesus gave his disciples shows that he felt the same for them; it is the same loving look that Jesus fixes on those he calls "my children." This all depicts discreetly, without repeating the word "love," how the love of Jesus for his disciples is also found in his look, and how all his tenderness is in the tone of his voice when he says, "my children."

Jesus speaks as if he was the father of the disciples, he who is the revelation of the heavenly Father.

On the Bosom of the Father

Lastly, in this skim through what Christ was able to reveal to his disciples about the tenderness of his Father, I would like to look briefly at a final expression to be found only in John's Gospel, which records not a saying but an attitude of Jesus. It is an expression of great sobriety which immerses us simply and wonderfully in the mystery of divine tenderness. Did all the disciples perceive what John felt? I don't know, but anyway it is John who takes care to open us up to mysteries.

As he narrates the Last Supper, John speaks to us, without naming him, of a disciple who is found "on the breast of Jesus" (13:23). John is circumspect as to the name of the disciple; it could be each of us. He has no need to say more; his desire is to take us further and lead us to contemplate what the attitude of Jesus reveals, and is infinitely more than just an expression of human tenderness. In fact, in the mere mention of this circumstance, John is simply repeating a term he has already used to describe the intimacy of the Father and the Son at the heart of the Trinity. "Nobody has seen God at any time, but the only Son, who is in the bosom of the Father, he has declared him to us" (1:18). That is enough; Jesus and his disciple on one hand, the Father and the Son on the other; in the simple bond of intimacy between Christ and his disciple, John was able to glimpse and contemplate the bond of tenderness that eternally unites the Father and the Son; it is a bottomless mystery to be revealed and contemplated in silence on the breast of Jesus.

> May you be exalted, Lord Jesus,
> For the immense peace,
> The blessed consolation,
> The wonderful rest
> Which you know how to give to those
> Who you welcome onto your breast!

> May you be exalted for the infinite tenderness
> With which you surround those you welcome this way
> With whom you share what you have received from your Father.

> Lord Jesus,
> You who are in the bosom of the Father,
> In the silence of the Holy Spirit,
> May you be exalted for receiving us so with tenderness
> to the very heart of the Holy Trinity,
> into the infinite depths of the mystery of humble love!

— CHAPTER 4 —

Infinite Tenderness

(Isaiah 25:6–9)

⁶ The Lord of the universe will prepare for all peoples, on this mountain, a feast of succulent dishes, a feast of vintage wines, of succulent meats full of marrow, of pure vintage wines. ⁷ On this mountain he will destroy the veil that is spread over all the peoples and the covering that covers all nations. ⁸ He will destroy death forever. The Lord God will wipe away the tears from every face; he will cause the reproach of his people to disappear from all the earth, because the Lord has spoken. ⁹ And it will be said in that day, "Behold, this is our God in whom we have hoped; it is he who saves us. It is he, the Lord, he in whom we have hoped. Let us be glad and rejoice in his salvation!"

UNLIKE THE ORACLES TRANSMITTED by Jeremiah and Ezekiel it is not God who speaks here. God is only present in the third person, without our being told the least word from him. God is totally silent. But on the other hand he is not inactive, far from it; the only actions depicted in the oracle are those of God.

All the actions described here are future, as prophecies, and the one who announces them to us and is not named is most certainly the prophet in person, Isaiah.

The Final Feast

The first thing announced to us as being undertaken by God is the preparation of a feast, in a place designated as "on this mountain." The mountain in question is easily identified, having been named in the last verse of the preceding chapter, Zion, the mountain of Jerusalem (24:23). God is going to provide a banquet in Jerusalem, in the very city he has chosen in the earth as a holy and sanctified place, the place without equal where he will meet with people.

The feast to come will take place at a time referred to as "in that day" (v. 9). This expression seems at first quite imprecise but in fact is very clear in the prophetic writings; it unequivocally designates the day of the final revelation of God, that is to say, the last day, the day that will see time tip into eternity.

Those invited to the feast of God are identified very clearly; they are, "all peoples," "all nations," not only the people of God, but really all the nations of the earth. The entirety of humanity is invited by God to the feast at the end of time.

In verse 10, we seem to find an exception to the list of invitees, Moab, who "will be trampled like straw in a pile of manure . . . the Lord will humble their pride." Is there going to be a people excluded when we have just read that "all" the nations will be among the guests? I believe that Moab is not here to be considered as a people.[1] In fact, all the peoples—those known at the time of course—including Moab, have been passed in review, each one receiving an oracle in chapters 13–23 of this book. Moab received its oracle (in chapter 15) along with the other nations. If Moab is mentioned again here, I believe it is not as a nation as such, but as a symbol of another reality. The description here makes Moab a symbol of pride; Moab is pride personified, so that is what God neither invites nor welcomes to his feast; pride has no place at God's banquet. In fact, it is to be destroyed; as such we are

1. The Lord, speaking through Jeremiah, did in fact promise a post-destruction recovery for the actual nation of Moab (Jer 48:47). (Trans.)

all involved. We are all invited to the feast, but knowing that we will have to leave our pride in the cloakroom and allow ourselves to be re-clothed in the humility of God. The feast is one of humility, from whatever nation we may be, whether already believers or not, loving God or humbly discovering him in that day.

During the feast, many things described in this oracle will take place; they will all be accomplished by God. God does not say anything during the feast but performs a number of actions, and these are described to us as actions that go much further than any words. The only ones to speak at the feast are the guests, as we see at the end of the oracle. They speak after seeing the work of God, when their joy will reach its peak. Everything that God does will fill the nations with joy and they will be united in their praise. "It will be said" (v. 9); this indefinite expression takes in all nations. "It will be said in that day; Behold, this is our God . . . It is him, the Lord." What is it that will cause the guests to acknowledge the undeniable lordship of God? What will God do during the feast to be acknowledged and accepted by all the nations as their God?

The Destruction of the
Veil and the Covering

God, the text tells us, will begin by lifting the veil, and in the same way the covering that covers all nations. I believe the veil and the covering are here considered a double reality that prevent the guests from seeing. The veil and the covering are interposed between God and the people in such a way that God cannot be seen, for two differing reasons. A veil, in effect, partially obstructs the view, whereas a covering obscures it entirely. Exactly what is this about?

I suggest that the veil and the covering be considered as two realities we have already discussed at length. The veil seems to me to designate the divine, self-effacing modesty, which God himself places between us and him, so as not to allow the reality and depth of his love and tenderness to be completely seen. All through human history God has used this veil of his modesty to only allow his love to be known partially. Here we are told that on the last day, from the start of the great banquet, God will allow the tenderness of his love to shine into the eyes of everyone.

The covering that completely prevents us from seeing God, it seems to me, is none other than our sin, which so obstructs our sight that we are absolutely incapable of contemplating God in all the beauty of his tenderness. If the veil is the mystery of his modesty, which God stretches out between us, the covering is something we spread ourselves, our profound darkness in which we obstinately refuse to fix our gaze on the mystery of God. Now God is going to destroy all that, to release our sight and allow us to contemplate him openly, face to face. Then all of us, believers and unbelievers, with full sight of God, will be able to say together, "Behold, this is our God . . . It is he, the Lord. Let us be glad and rejoice in his salvation!"

The Destruction of Death

After freeing our sight from everything that obstructs it, God will perform a second act every bit as wonderful, one which concerns us all, believers as much as unbelievers: "he will destroy death forever." We humans are capable of pushing death away for a while, we can postpone it, but God alone is able to destroy it. Such an event certainly situates us at the end of time, on the threshold of eternity. As the apostle Paul tells us, death is the final enemy of God (1 Cor 15:26). Here, with the destruction of this last enemy, this curse of the human race, the whole of humanity will be able to participate in this feast as in an eternal celebration, on the mountain of Zion, i.e., at the very place where the crucified one vanquished death. "Then it will be said by all, both by believers and the unbelievers who will discover it, Behold, it is he, our God . . . It is he, the Lord. Let us be glad and rejoice in his salvation!"

In salvation history there are two crucial moments that should not be confused; that of victory over death, which took place at the cross, and that of the destruction of death, which will take place at the end of time. The biblical texts speak now of one, now of the other, and at times of both. If a text speaks of one of these moments without mentioning the other, this takes nothing away from the one that is not mentioned. Here, the prophet speaks of the destruction of death and says nothing of the victory won on the cross, but we should not conclude that he dismisses this as unimportant; we have only to read Isaiah 53 to see that this is not so. The victory over death is the work of the Son; its destruction, the work of the Father. The oracle of Isaiah 25 centers on the work of the Father, which detracts nothing from the work of the Son accomplished on the cross.

Announcement of Infinite Tenderness _____

After the almighty action taken by God against death—death, which causes so many tears to flow, among believers and unbelievers alike—after this, God's guests will behold an action that is perhaps unexpected, an action on which we will now focus, the expression of an overwhelming tenderness; "God will wipe away the tears from every face . . . " This is an infinite tenderness surpassing anything the feast-goers might have expected, a tenderness that plunges them into an amazed silence before letting loose the eternal cry of praise . . . "Behold, this is our God . . . It is he, the Lord. Let us be glad and rejoice in his salvation!"

Reader friend, silence already grips me just thinking about this action of God, so what will it be then, when we see him tenderly wipe away the tears from every face . . . ? I have meditated on this phrase for years, and I am always quite overcome.

Everyone might hope, more or less in secret, to see death disappear, but how many of us here below have thought that God himself might set about wiping away our tears . . . ?

How many tears has death caused to be shed, and how many more will it cause in all nations, among believers and non-believers? Are not the tears of both groups all just the same? How overpowering it will be for us all when we see God himself go round the guests and draw near to each one to wipe away their tears. "Then, in that day, we will say with one accord, Behold, this is our God . . . It is he, the Lord. Let us be glad and rejoice in his salvation!"

The Announcement Repeated Twice

This act of tenderness on God's part so struck readers of the book of Isaiah that it is recalled and repeated in the book of Revelation, not just once, but twice, showing the extent to which this prophecy has touched hearts. These two passages are also transnational in context and concern the end times.

The first time God's action is announced is in the opening part of the Revelation, in a passage (7:13–17) that we should read through:

> [13] One of the elders began to speak and said to me, "These here of every nation and every tribe, dressed in white, who are they, and where do they come from?" [14] I said to him, "Sir, you know." Then he said to me, "These are they who come out of the great tribulation; they have washed their robes white in the blood of the lamb. [15] That is why they appear before the throne of God and serve him day and night in his temple. He who is seated on the throne will spread his tent over them; [16] they will never hunger or thirst again and neither the sun nor any burning heat will overcome them. [17] Because the lamb in the center of the throne will feed them and lead them to the fountains of the water of life, and God will wipe away every tear from their eyes."

The second passage is found nearly at the end of the Revelation (21:1–4), and the end time dimension is still more evident:

> ¹ Then I saw a new heaven and a new earth, because the first heaven and the first earth had passed away, and the sea was no more. ² I saw descend from heaven, from God, the Holy City, the new Jerusalem, prepared as a bride who has dressed herself for the bridegroom. ³ Then I heard a loud voice from the throne which said, "Behold, the dwelling place of God is with people! He will live with them, and they will be his people and God himself will be with them. ⁴ He will wipe away every tear from their eyes, and death will be no more, and there shall be no more pain or crying or sorrow, because the former things are passed away."

Closer and Closer

All of this serves to reinforce what is already in the book of Isaiah. In these three passages there is an action God accomplishes without saying anything, in silence; in each passage it is not God himself who announces what he does. Each time we learn it from the mouth of someone else, and each time the someone else is different. The three testimonies are different but concordant and all three are given us by those we can consider confidants of God. After all, who but a confidant could announce such a thing?

In Isaiah, God's action is announced by the prophet himself, very much a confidant of God, like all the prophets.

In Revelation 7, the action is announced by "one of the elders," which is to say, not by a person on earth like Isaiah, but a heavenly person, one of the twenty-four elders seated on thrones near the throne of God (4:4). Here too, these are confidants of God.

In Revelation 21, the action is announced by "a loud voice coming from the throne [of God]." Whose is this voice that speaks for God without actually being his? Nobody, in any case, could be closer to God than whoever speaks in this way. Who is it then?

It could be one of the four living beings that the Revelation positions "in the center of the throne and around the throne" (4:6). It is possible that it might be one of these who speaks, but we can also understand it another way, and that is the line I will pursue. The passage in chapter 7 we have just read teaches, among other passages, that on the very throne of God is the sacrificial lamb (7:17), that is to say, Christ himself (3:21). It is then he, the Son, who announces to us from the throne of God what the Father will do, which helps us to understand that the one who will wipe away our tears is none other than God the Father.

The prophet from the earth, one of the elders from heaven and finally Christ himself from the very throne of his Father, these are the confidants who one by one speak and announce to us what the Father will do, and what the Father himself has never stated in his modest reserve.

The three announcements are made to us by a confidant who on each occasion is in closer and closer proximity to God, and this gives rise in us to a growing confidence to welcome the announcement as an ever more assured truth, a truth to be considered with increasing attention. What Christ did not take time to tell us during his earthly ministry, he now tells us from the throne in heaven, which is to say with an authority that gives it a credibility and force which could not be greater.

More on the Maternal Father

We will now examine this revelation given to us by a prophet, an elder, and then also by the Son regarding his Father and what he will bring to pass during the last feast.

"To wipe away the tears." This expression is very visual and invites us to somehow picture God acting it out. God is unseen, but we should try all the same to enter into this scene, which cannot be understood without some attempt visualization. May the Lord open the eyes of our heart to enable us to enter into contemplation of this mystery.

To wipe away someone's tears, not your own, but those of another; who on earth apart from God has done such a thing? Nowhere else in the rest of the Bible do we see anyone wipe away the tears of another; there is no biblical reference that can help us understand this action in its depth. We will therefore have to lean upon our human experience, our own experience. I think we can say that it is very exceptional to see an adult wipe away the tears of another adult because, in general, we wipe away our own tears. What, on the other hand, is quite common is to see a father, or even more often a mother, wipe away the tears of their child, because children often just forget to do this, and will even at times come looking for it as a gesture of comfort from their mother. So it is, it seems to me, a gesture that is essentially paternal or maternal, and we can easily see that, in acting this way, God is present as a maternal Father, as we have already discussed at length. The tenderness expressed in this act fully reveals what other texts have already shown us; God, the maternal Father.

This maternal Father will allow his infinite tenderness to be seen before the eyes of all; we will be both witnesses and beneficiaries since we will see God wipe away the tears of others and we will see him approach us with the same tenderness to wipe away our tears . . . What a wonder! The whole earth will be immersed in the wonderment that already takes hold of us as we merely picture what is announced here.

Many people have told me that they never cry. I can accept that, but who never cried as a child? And who could not weep with emotion before such a scene as this? Surely, though, isn't God also well able to wipe away our unshed, interior tears? Jeremiah was among those who have wept copiously, but he tells us that he feels that his soul is also able to cry. "If you do not listen, my soul will weep in secret, and my eyes will run down with tears" (13:17). It is true; the eyes can cry, but the soul can too at times, and the tears of the soul are of an altogether different depth. They may escape the eyes of others, but they don't escape God, who, in his tenderness, is coming to wipe them away.

Many Ways to Console

To wipe away someone's tears is clearly an act of consolation, but we should remind ourselves that it is not the only way of comforting someone. If this particular action is reserved by God for the end, this does not mean, happily, that God is waiting until then to console us. God surely has many ways to console and comfort, today! The present reality of God's consolation is beyond doubt. Yes, God consoles us, as is repeated over and over in the book of Isaiah—as a present reality. "It is I, it is I who comfort you," he tells us with feeling (51:12, cf. 49:13; 51:3; 52:9). Clearly, God comforts us in various ways, always with the same tenderness, but the wiping away of tears is reserved till the end.

In the majority of the biblical passages that affirm that God consoles, this is not done with images or details that explain how he does it, but that is not important; what is important is to know that essentially it is by *words* that God consoles. You will have discovered this; it is God's words that really comfort us. One beautiful expression synonymous with "console" that is very helpful here is the expression "to speak to the heart." Joseph consoles his brothers by speaking to the heart (Gen 50:21); Boaz consoles Ruth in the same way (Ruth 2:13). It's what God wants done to comfort Jerusalem (Isa 40:1), and what he prepares himself to do to comfort his well-beloved (Hos 2:16). Indeed, words of consolation are those that touch the heart; so it is by his word that God most commonly brings us consolation today.

A word of comfort does not necessarily need to be accompanied by action to be more effective, but it could also be that some action accompanies the word or even replaces it; with God an action alone can console, as we see in this action, which entirely surpasses words. Are there any other acts of consolation? Certainly, yes. I can point to a very beautiful text, full of tenderness, indeed of maternal tenderness, applied by God to himself, one not reserved for the end times. "You will be carried in my arms and dandled upon my knees. Like a child comforted by his mother, so I will comfort you" (Isa 66:12–13). This action, unaccompanied by speech, is very close to the one we are considering. The comfort here is in maternal caresses, but without specifying whether the caresses go so far as wiping away tears. That might be implied, but is not clearly stated.

With Open Face

To wipe away someone's tears is an act that implies very great intimacy, an extreme intimacy that goes well beyond all we might think of our relationship with God; how close God is, how wonderfully close, coming to brush our cheeks with his hand! This is a gesture that goes beyond our understanding because no one in the Bible is described as being so close to God, so close as to offer him his face and allow God to put his hand to their cheeks to wipe away tears.

A person who offers his cheeks to the hand of God as a child would, is surely presenting himself before God with an uncovered face; this is simply unthinkable in the Bible. I will explain.

When someone finds themselves in the presence of God, the first reaction is to hide their face simply to avoid seeing God, because anyone who sees God face to face would surely die, since the glory of God's face is not something human eyes can bear. When Elijah realizes he is in God's presence he immediately covers his face (1 Kgs 19:13). The seraphim, close as they are to God, cover their faces in his presence (Isa 6:2). Who would dare present himself with uncovered face before God for him to wipe away their tears?

If the face is unveiled, the reaction is to prostrate oneself, face to the ground, which comes to the same thing. This is how Moses prostrated himself when he knew he was in the presence of God (Exod 34:8). The same goes for the twenty-four elders of the Revelation (4:10), as also the four living creatures, although even closer to God (Rev 19:4).

Someone in tears before God would never show him those tears! And if we were told that he was going to come near to wipe away our tears, which of us would dare to stand without hiding his face? Who would claim to be in closer intimacy than Moses or Elijah, or even than the seraphim and elders in heaven?

What is going to happen during the feast of all nations that will enable the guests to dare to present their tears to God? Surely, God must be going to adopt an attitude such that everyone, pagans included, will feel so intimate and confident as to open themselves, faces uncovered, to the comfort of God. I find it infinitely difficult to imagine this, far beyond my understanding. Nevertheless, this is really what is announced here, "he will wipe away the tears from every face"!

Incomparable Humility

If all this is way over our heads, it may be that we need to change something in our way of thinking about God, and, it seems to me, on a rather precise point. For God to approach his guests in this way during the feast without anyone veiling their face, I believe it necessary for God to be particularly humble, incomparably humble.

Here I recall a Gospel text that helps me to understand, a text that describes an attitude in Jesus of extreme humility. Who could better renew our understanding of the Father? It is in seeing the humility of Christ that we can glimpse that of the Father. On one particular day, during a meal in fact, a meal he was presiding over, Jesus left the table to wash the feet of his guests. He so humbled himself before them that he obliged them to look down to see their Master at their feet. Then, as he lifted his face to speak to them, they would each have seen him face to face, he lower than they. If they had had tears in their eyes, the humble man at their feet could easily have wiped them away without any of them hiding his face. True, Jesus did not on this occasion wipe away tears from the disciples, but everything was set up for it.

Through this extreme attitude of humility, I believe that Christ prepares us to meet the Father, who, on the day of the feast, will perhaps do the same, so that we need not turn away when he draws near to remove our tears. Only the extreme humility of the Son can reveal to us the extreme humility of the Father. Reader friend, tell me, what would stop the Father during the last feast, from rising from the table, stooping humbly before each guest to wash their feet and then wipe the tears away from their face, without anyone thinking of hiding their face? I believe him quite capable of it.

The Final Act

John, the seer of Revelation, begins to weep when he is in the presence of the throne of God (5:4). An elder approaches and tries to stop the tears, saying simply, "Don't weep," but neither he nor anyone else makes as if to wipe the tears away. It was not yet time.

Jesus himself saw plenty of tears fall, but he didn't wipe any away. He saw the widow at Nain weeping, but merely invited her to stop crying; he didn't wipe away her tears. He saw Jairus and his wife cry (Luke 8:52), but he didn't wipe away their tears. He saw Mary of Bethany cry at the tomb of her brother Lazarus (John 11:33), but he didn't wipe away her tears. Early in the morning of Easter day he saw Mary Magdalene cry (John 20:13), but he didn't wipe away her tears either.

Jesus never did this, no doubt because it was not yet time, and no doubt also because no one was ready for an act of such intimacy; also no doubt because his sense of modesty forbade it; but above all, it seems to me, because of his immense and humble respect for his Father. I believe that he abstained from wiping tears away in order to reserve this act of such great tenderness for his Father and for him alone, and also so that one day he himself may marvel, watching his Father wipe away our tears.

To watch the Father wiping tears away from every face could not but birth in us an immense tenderness towards him. We will then be overwhelmed with this tenderness and in an instant our hearts, until then so hard and insensitive to the tenderness of God, will become soft and tender. We will be transformed in our hearts by this act alone, and our innermost beings moved with tenderness. The tenderness that God has never laid claim to for himself will then be given. "It will be said in that day, Behold, this is our God! It is he, the Lord! Let us be glad and rejoice in his salvation."

When All Reserve Disappears

If God waits until the last day to act like this, it is because modest reserve will still be present. If Jesus did not wipe away tears from the faces, it is for this reason too. But on the last day, God himself will cause the veil of modesty to disappear because it will have no more reason to exist. What is it that will make it unnecessary? This, it seems to me, is the moment to try to understand the nature of the modesty, the reserve, the delicacy, and why it is needed here on earth but will be redundant at the end of time.

Modesty is a veil that attempts to hide something beautiful. It has nothing in common with shame or hypocrisy; they also seek to hide something, not what is beautiful and honorable, but what is bad, blameworthy, things we don't wish to acknowledge. Modesty seeks to hide what is beautiful because beauty is fragile and vulnerable. It hides to protect what might be damaged, wounded by others. If modesty veils tenderness, it is because tenderness is vulnerable and can be wounded.

In itself, tenderness has no defense; it has no other recourse than to the veil of modesty for protection. This tells us how vulnerable it is. Even the tenderness of God is vulnerable. It can be the object of contempt or mockery, which wound it. It is like Christ, without defense, delivered up to the torturers who slap him, whip him, and spit in his face.

Modesty veils, essentially to protect from certain types of look; there are looks that do harm, looks that wound, as you well know, probably to your cost.

Voyeurism hurts; it both wounds and defiles. Faced with this, it is best to hide any tenderness to preserve it. The more beautiful and deep the tenderness, the more we must protect it from prying eyes.

A look of covetousness also wounds tenderness, and again is protected against by modesty. A covetous look dirties and sullies whatever it sets its eyes upon.

There are also looks of disrespect, looks without love, of disdain, of jealousy, of mockery, looks of derision. All these soil and wound profoundly, so that modesty must always be interposed with great care to protect tenderness in its vulnerable fragility. It will be so on earth, just so long as people are capable of such attitudes, and that will unfortunately be so until the last day. But on that last day there will be no more reason for modesty because God will do away with every trace of lust, mockery, derision, jealousy, contempt, disrespect . . . which is to say, he will have transformed us. God will transform the expressions on our faces as well as our hearts in such a way that we can look at our fellow guests at the feast without hurting others, not even the most fragile of them and no longer wounding the humble tenderness of God.

When our transformed gazes meet that of God, what will we see in his eyes? We will see his unfathomable tenderness and contemplate it eternally. An endless mystery . . . ! "It will be said in that day, Behold, this is our God! It is he, the Lord! Let us be glad and rejoice in his salvation!"

All that I say about the tenderness of God is no more than stammering, it goes so far beyond, so far above my understanding. What I can say is that it will be freely opened to our sight after death has been destroyed. This simply means that death will not be the last word in history; the last word will be the tenderness of God; death is only for a while, but tenderness is eternal . . . how wonderful!

All Tears

"God will wipe away tears from all faces"; this expression in Isaiah is recalled twice in Revelation, but with a small difference that merits our attention, because, without contradicting what is already in the Isaiah statement, it underlines its implications.

On both occasions, Revelation says, "God will wipe away all tears from their eyes." The mention of faces is replaced by eyes, which to my mind is not a great difference. By contrast, the adjective "all" has been moved and is now applied not to the faces, but to the tears, which has the effect of underlining the range of different tears. *"Every* tear"; this is what God will take such care to wipe away, and from *every* face.

"Every tear"; how necessary! As soon as we think about it we realize that tears have an amazing diversity and that each of us during our lives may shed a great range of them. Here we are told that God will wipe away each of these tears, of whatever type. It would be difficult to make a full inventory of tears, so I will just suggest a few to help us better marvel at the scope at God's deed.

The mention of death in the Isaiah oracle, as well as in the second passage in Revelation, points to tears of mourning, revealing God as the perfect comforter of the bereaved. That much is clear but these will not be the only tears on the faces of guests at the last feast. "Every tear" highlights their great range.

Innocent Tears

Of course, there are the tears of children, ranging from the most tragic to the most inconsequential, those a child might cry over nothing and those in situations of great drama. The baby Moses cried in his basket, calling for his mother (Exod 2:6); he seemed to have been abandoned, which was not in fact the case. There are also those children who have really been abandoned or orphaned, who have no mother or father to comfort them. God will draw near to each child to wipe the tears away.

There are children who refuse to be comforted by their parents; perhaps their parents are separated or divorced and they show their resentment against a situation they consider unjust. There are children who have been abused, who wait for a consolation that never comes. God will take time to wipe away all these tears.

All these children are innocent, no doubt; they will attract the infinite compassion of God who will wipe away their tears with all his tenderness. But it is not only innocent children who cry; there are also innocent parents who weep their tears more or less silently, but always in sorrow. I think of Rachel, who is said to be inconsolable over the loss of her children (Jer 31:15). As you know, that short oracle is recalled in Matthew's Gospel in relation to the massacre of innocents ordered by Herod, to indicate the tears of the mothers, also innocent, weeping for their children massacred by the tyrant (2:16–18). How many mothers today, far from Bethlehem, are inconsolable after losing a child killed by some psychopath, or a tyrant, by an alcoholic or a pervert . . . In his tenderness God will draw near to silently wipe away all these innocent tears.

There are also the tears of Jacob, believing his son dead and feeling that he is beyond comfort (Gen 37:35), just as there are tears of compassion shed by Job's friends to console him in his grief (Job 2:12). They were also innocent, as was Job himself in his ill-fortune.

Among these innocents we could mention Jephthah's daughter, whose story you no doubt have read. Jephthah made a foolish vow to sacrifice the first person who would come to meet him if he could just return victorious from war. He was victorious and the first to approach him on his return was his only daughter. She asked of her father a delay of two months in order, she said, to "mourn her virginity" (Judg 11:37) How many tears would she have wept in those two months? How many young people are there today who are sacrificed by parents who make senseless choices? God will once again draw near to wipe away all such tears.

Also among innocent tears we should not forget the tears of all the handicapped, adults and children, who innocently weep over their handicaps, both physical and mental. God, again, will take care to draw near and wipe away these tears one by one with the tenderness of his compassion.

Guilty Tears

We do not only shed innocent tears; there also guilty tears, principally the tears of compunction that lead to repentance, shed while seeking pardon from God or from other people. Many of these are shed in secret, in shame or despair. Peter, of course, is the very example of those who, aware of their fault, shed tears of bitterness. These tears are all the more bitter given that Jesus himself was the object of his disciple's denial. When Peter leaves his place near the fire and retreats into the darkness, nobody wipes away the tears he sheds. But God himself, the Father of our Lord Jesus Christ, will arise and draw near to Peter to wipe his tears away with all the tenderness of his mercy.

On the day of the great feast, Peter will not be alone, but will be joined by all those who have shed tears in full awareness of their faults. The Bible doesn't say it, but no doubt Jephthah must have wept at the loss of his daughter; Cain perhaps would also have wept over his error after he murdered his brother; don't forget Judas either, Judas who repented, returning and throwing down in the temple the silver he had been paid (Matt 27:3–5). How many tears did he shed before wrapping a rope round his neck? I think again of Ephraim, who we saw grieving over the golden calf that had so wounded God. There's no doubt this confession was accompanied by tears, the tears of shame which are so bitter. Who in the past wiped away the tears of Jephthah, Cain, of Ephraim or Judas? God will draw near to each one and carefully wipe away with tenderness all tears, looking at each one, his eyes full of the gentleness of mercy.

So Many Other Tears

There are so many other tears that are neither really innocent nor really guilty, tears we have shed for all sorts of reasons; the tears of frustrated whims, tears of wounded self-love, tears of trampled vanity, as also tears of vexation, of failure, disappointment, anger, jealousy . . . how many more we could enumerate, the list is so long. In his tenderness God is going to come very close and wipe away all the tears without saying a word. There will be no need for him to say anything because we will be thoroughly aware of the futility of our whims, the poverty of our vanity, the foolishness of our pride . . . and if we continue to cry for shame, God will continue his act of comfort as if to say, "There is no need to speak!" His forgiveness will reconcile us with ourselves and with him. "Then, on that day, it will be said, This is our God! It is he, the Lord! Let us be glad and rejoice in his salvation!"

There are also tears that are shed because of all the divisions between people, countries fighting one another, divisions within families, between churches. There are tears Catholics have caused Protestants and tears Protestants have caused Catholics. I have seen plenty of these tears and shed some myself, but tell me, what is the difference between the tears of a Catholic and those of a Protestant? Aren't they the same? What is the difference between the tears of a black man and those of a white man? Between those of a Jew and those of a Muslim? They are all the same and there is no doubt at all that many more will flow. Before all the guests of all the nations assembled on Mount Zion, God will rise up and will surely wipe away every single tear, from every single person, with equal tenderness, that infinite tenderness which is able to reconcile all people with each another.

Tears That are Buried

I also think of other tears that need to be discussed, tears that are suppressed, held back, and that we try to bury, tears that we do not allow ourselves to shed because were we to do so we would simply collapse; these are the tears that we repress with all our strength, perhaps even from early childhood, and that we expect to keep down till the end of our days. In the presence of God these tears will well up of their own accord from the depths of the soul. Then God will come close in his infinite tenderness and spend as much time as is needed to wipe them away until a smile of recognition responds to his gentleness.

You see, reader friend, what an endless chapter we have opened, but we need to close it and move on. However, before putting a final close to it, I would like to look at another short text from the Egyptian desert concerning the beautiful Abba Poemen, whose tenderness we know. Here is what was said of him, which speaks for itself.

> Abba Joseph tells how Abba Isaac said the following. One day, when I was sitting near Abba Poemen, I saw him go into a trance. As I was very free with him, I bowed down before him and asked him, "tell me, where were you?" Self-consciously he said, "My thoughts were with Saint Mary, the mother of God; she was in tears as she stood by the cross of the Savior; and for me, I wish I could always be weeping this way." (*Apoph.* 718)

These tears will also be wiped away by God the Father; he will wipe away all tears shed on account of his Son. It is with the expectation of that day that Christ said, thinking of all, all the guests at the last feast, "Blessed are those who weep, for they shall be comforted."

We now need to spend a little more time on this action of God's and attempt to understand more of its meaning. It is an act that consoles, comforts, but much more, it is a consolation with many facets.

An Action That Saves and Heals

First of all, I would say that this action of God is an act that saves. I say this simply because it leads the guests at the great feast to say in their final acclamation, "This is our God, it is he who has saved us . . . let us rejoice in his salvation!" The insistence on the verb "save," repeated in the noun "salvation," shows that the guests perceive the comfort of God as marking the end of their slavery. How many slaves weep over their lost liberty, over their bondage! How many alcoholics chained to the bottle weep over it in their moments of lucidity! Surely the rich young man, a prisoner of his money, must have wept in his sadness after walking away from Christ! Don't all our inner enslavements, to anger or jealousy or any other passion, cause our tears to fall? When God wipes away all our tears, we will understand that this action marks our liberation. Then we too will join the eternal praise, "Behold, this is our God, he who has saved us . . . let us rejoice in his salvation!"

In Hebrew, the word "to save" also means "to heal," and we need to bear this in mind if we are to better understand the intent of the eternal acclamation uttered by the guests at the great feast. "It is he who has healed us . . . let us rejoice in his healing!" It means that as he wipes away our tears, our God, our wonderful therapist, will lead us to understand that we are healed of all the infirmities that have made us weep, physical infirmities as well as mental or spiritual. God will wipe the tears away from everyone he will have healed.

An Action That Rehabilitates and Sanctifies _____

This action of God is also an action that rehabilitates. This meaning comes out clearly from the first text in Revelation that we read. The passage presents a multitude dressed in white, who, the elder tells us, comprise all those "who have come out of the great tribulation." It is from these, he says, that God will wipe away tears. The "great tribulation" indicates persecutions undergone for God's sake, with their load of suffering endured under the oppression of forces of evil. The struggles of the spiritual life are indicated here, and this concerns Christians, but also, perhaps, Muslims and Jews or others who suffer for God. Tell me, reader friend, in these spiritual battles, by whom are the tears shed? The victors no doubt shed tears of joy, but that is nothing beside the vanquished, who are more numerous and shed an abundance of tears over their unhappy defeats. This group will also be there, coming out of the great tribulation, also dressed in white, but their eyes filled with bitter tears.

We have made a custom in the church of honoring victors; we display their names on our calendars. But what of the others? All those who have been beaten and have fallen, they will be there among the guests on the day of the great feast. Well, God will draw near to them too to wipe away their tears. The tenderness of God is also for the rehabilitation of the defeated.

This might be surprising, but we could also say that God's act is also an act that sanctifies. Here is why: throughout the Bible holiness is transmitted by contact; it is enough for an offering to be placed on the altar of the temple in Jerusalem for it to become holy through its contact with that which is holy (see Matt 23:19). In the same way when God wipes away the tears from the faces, the touch of his hand will be enough to sanctify. On the holy mountain, where God will prepare the feast on the last day, all the guests will be sanctified by the touch of the hand of the thrice Holy who will wipe away their tears. All the victors who have been canonized by the church will be joined together with those who were defeated, who God will have rehabilitated and sanctified. "Then it will be said, in that day, this is our God, he in whom we have trusted; it is he who saves us . . ."

An Action That Converts

Finally, among the different meanings contained in God's action there is one that demands attention. I would say quite simply of this action that it is one that converts. I say this, thinking of the great number of non-believers who will be found among the guests and who are designated by the term "the nations"; in the Bible, "the nations" means "pagans" or gentiles. They are described here as equally having over them the covering that God will destroy, thereby doing away with all that impedes the non-believer from seeing God or even thinking that he exists. God will free them from this covering of darkness, and at the end of the feast they will break out into praises, saying with the believers, "Behold, this is our God!" What is it that will tip them from unbelief into faith? Well, quite simply, they will have seen God draw near to others and to them, to humbly wipe away their tears. They will have discovered the unspeakable tenderness of God, the infinite tenderness of his compassion and mercy. They will have seen God at work in his tenderness; they will have seen and experienced this tenderness. There will be no need for God to speak, his silent action will be enough, an action directed not at the intellect but the heart; one action alone and they will all confess the lordship of God and to proclaim that he is henceforth their God—"Behold, this is our God . . . !"

Then they will add, and indeed repeat, a phrase that challenges me greatly; they add, "we have hoped in him," "we have waited for him." This means that though they may not have believed in God, they had nevertheless hoped in him, without ever having said so, or having encountered him before this last day when God makes himself known to them in his tenderness. What they had hoped for, in the end, is a God of tenderness. If they had never yet encountered him, no doubt it is because no one from among the believers had introduced them to this God, this Father of such tenderness. No doubt they would have heard speeches on the subject of God, but never such as to convince because not fashioned by the tenderness of God. Had they perhaps never met believers indwelt by the tenderness of God? Oh, dear reader friend, may the Lord forgive us and root deeply within us the evidence they need. It is enough for God, with the overwhelming power of his tenderness, to wipe the tears away from those who weep for the non-believers to begin to say, "Behold, this is our God, in whom we had hoped . . ."

Reader friend, don't let us wait until the end of time to testify about God as he is revealed to us here, with his endless tenderness; non-believers are hoping for him, secretly no doubt, without telling us, and perhaps without even admitting it to themselves. We mustn't wait until the end, because in every person, in every person, there is a thirst for tenderness that can never be sated until they find God as their source, the source from which a tenderness flows to wonderfully quench the thirst of all. Let us not wait until the end to speak because the world also thirsts for witnesses to this kind of God, witnesses to speed on the coming day.

An Action That Fulfils

The first true witness who didn't wait until the end to testify is Jesus himself. His whole life is a witness offered to the tenderness of the Father, an embodiment of the tenderness of God. There is a witness right in the cross, in his final prayer, "Father, forgive them, they know not what they do" (Luke 23:34).

"Father," or as he would have said, "Abba" (Mark 14:36); all the tenderness of the Son for the Father is in this one word, prayed one more time on the cross in all the humility, fragility, and destitution of the one who has nothing but tenderness for his Father and for us.

"Forgive them, they know not what they do." This prayer over-flows with an infinite tenderness for us, for us who, like the disciples, deny him, betray him, or abandon him; or who, like the crowd, the soldiers, and the rulers, wound him, slap him, whip and crucify him . . . "Father, forgive them, they don't know what they have done, they don't know the extent to which they wounded you in the tenderness of your love for me and for them; yes, Father, forgive them . . ."

How does the Father respond to this prayer of the Son? He receives it in his infinite tenderness, welcomes it and fulfils it, beyond indeed what is asked of him. Not only does he forgive, but more; on that last day he will draw near to wipe away the tears of each of us who in one way or another has participated in the death of Christ. This final action of God's will then appear to us as the fulfillment of the Son's prayer. This act of tenderness fulfils the prayer of tenderness; "yes, my well-beloved Son, I do forgive them; I comfort them, wiping away their tears . . ."

Reader friend, let us not wait until the end to take our turn as witnesses in this world; don't wait until the end to pray with Christ that the Holy Spirit would so mold our hearts that we are full of tenderness towards the Father, saying to him, "Father, forgive us!" Don't wait till the end to pray, full of tenderness for all humanity, including in our prayer both believers and non-believers, "Father, forgive us, we don't know what we do, we don't know the degree to which we grieve you or the degree to which we grieve your Son!" We should pray this way without ceasing, right up to the day when we see the Father rise up and humbly draw near to all the guests, to wipe away the tears from every face, humbly, in silence, with infinite tenderness.

Time to Get Ready

Before drawing to a close, I would like to engage you in a question that the reading of this oracle in Isaiah presses upon me and that continues to concern me. Maybe the question is impertinent or false; I hope not. It plunges me into lengthy reflection. It is this: why does God wait until the end of time to wipe away the tears from every face? It is such a simple act, so beautiful and great, so convincing that it alone is enough for him to touch every heart, even those of non-believers; why then wait so long to do it? There are so many tears on this earth that no one has ever wiped away and that no one ever will; why then wait?

Certainly I discard out of hand anything that suggests there might be in God some shade of sadism. This would be utter blasphemy and I strongly resist any such thought; if God is waiting till that last day to wipe away tears, he nevertheless doesn't wait for the end to bring comfort to those who weep. He doesn't delay, as we have seen; from the beginning and still today, God is so compassionate and merciful that he takes great pains to comfort, mainly through words of consolation that touch the heart, because they are spoken "to the heart." God does not wait for the end to bring comfort, that is clear; nevertheless, he does wait to perform this final act—to wipe away tears.

Why then? Here is the answer I have and now share; if God waits it is to allow us time to get ready, to prepare ourselves. We should recognize that we are not ready to see God wipe away our tears or those of others. God is ready, but we are not. I say this because this action of God has about it an immense mystery, or even, it seems to me, many mysteries; I can only suggest these now and they are no more than suggestions because a mystery can only be suggested and contemplated, never analyzed. I believe that we will be able to experience this act of God's more intensely when we have savored the taste of mystery a little more. His act is too profound for us to be able to experience more than superficially. In his grace, God allows us time to more deeply prepare ourselves.

The Mystery of Tears _____

The great feast announced by the prophet will unfold in Jerusalem; this seems an important point to note and consider. Jerusalem is the city where Jesus saw many tears fall, as reported by Luke in his account of the Passion. As he carried his cross towards Golgotha, Jesus met some women who were weeping, mourning over him. He told them, "Daughters of Jerusalem, don't weep for me but weep for yourselves and for your children!" (23:28). Jesus made no attempt to comfort the women and he didn't wish to stop them weeping. Instead he invited them to shed their tears for others and not for him; "Weep for yourselves and for your children."

Why propose that these women weep even more? Because they would discover a mystery in the tears they shed over Jerusalem. "Daughters of Jerusalem, weep for yourselves and for your children, until you discover that someone has already wept for you and for your children." Jesus' invitation to the women was aimed at opening their hearts to the fact that he himself had wept over Jerusalem, as the same Gospel of Luke tells us (19:41). To underline this connection, Luke reports what Jesus said at that moment. He wept because of the evil hour that was coming to Jerusalem; more precisely, he said to the city, "Your enemies will destroy you and your children" (19:44). If Jesus is now encouraging the women of Jerusalem to weep for themselves and for their children, it is to make them understand that mixed with their tears are his own tears, which he too had wept over them and their children.

The first mystery that presents itself here is that the tears of Jesus are blended with ours. Before he wipes away our tears, God allows us time to discover that Christ comes alongside to share them. When we shed tears of repentance he comes in his tenderness to weep in repentance with us. When we shed innocent tears, he again comes in his tenderness to weep with us. When we shed tears of compassion, he comes in his tenderness to share these too. In this way all our bitter tears find their consolation in his. How deep is this mystery, this communion of love we find in the tears that Jesus sheds with us! What depth of love and tenderness on the part of the Son! If the Father is waiting before wiping away our tears, it is to allow us time to discover the tenderness with which his Son informs our tears, when he comes to weep with us.

We know that when a loved one comes and shares our tears and cries with us, there is no need to say anything; in the tears we receive a sweet consolation. To weep with a loved one is to comfort them. I became really aware of this when, one day, as a young pastor, I went to visit a woman who was to undergo a serious operation. I had arrived at the hospital just as her husband was leaving her room. As soon as I was with the woman I mentioned her husband's visit, and she said to me with an immense sense of release, "His visit did me so much good because he wept with me, and this is the first time I have ever seen him cry!" This is the mystery of compassion, which makes bitter tears sweet when they are shared, a mystery that is extraordinarily enlightening on the day we discover that Jesus comes to mix his tears with ours.

All this requires time; the time to discover, in the concrete reality of our lives, how our bitter tears are sweetened from the moment we realize that Christ weeps with us. When we have entered into this mystery of love communion with the Son, then the Father will be able to draw near and wipe away the tears of sorrow, which become sweet tears of love.

To discover and live concretely out of the tenderness of Christ requires time! It calls for a lengthy journey, not a cerebral one, but a journey of the heart. On this journey I believe that the apostle Paul was well along the way when he wrote to the Philippians, "I cherish you with the tenderness of Jesus Christ" (1:8). To write this way, Paul had to have taken time to allow the tenderness of Christ to live in him, to become blended with his. This is the pathway open before us and along which the Father gives us time to advance.

Even These Tears _____

If God still waits and gives us time to prepare, it is without doubt for another reason, which touches on another mystery; I would like to merely suggest this now, such is its depth.

If someone comes to wipe away your tears and you accept this gesture because you know it to be full of love, you will do nothing to lower your head or turn away; you cannot help holding up your face to the other and sooner or later, to look at him, fix your eyes on him. Now, tell me, when God comes to do this for you, won't you be face to face before him, looking him in the eye? This is where we find the endless mystery. What will you see in those eyes? Reader friend, you will be able to see the tears he has shed for you! Then you will really know what eternity is. Heaven and earth will be silent and you will be immersed in an unfathomable mystery, immersed in the infinite mystery of a love and tenderness far beyond my words.

Perhaps you remember the words God spoke one day to Jeremiah? As I remind you, I am endeavoring to invest each word with its full weight of love. "You will say to them these words; 'tears run down from my eyes night and day without ceasing, because my daughter, this young virgin, has been beaten with a heavy blow'" (14:17). What Jeremiah didn't see, you will contemplate: you will see God's tears falling . . . What a mystery of love and tenderness! I can hardly even imagine what it is that I am saying, but wouldn't you agree that we need time to get ready to experience this moment of eternity when we look into the heart of such mystery. Jeremiah himself was not ready and God only informed him; he only spoke to him of the mystery of his tears, but without allowing him to see them. What he said to him was to allow us to prepare, but there is no one among us who is ready yet, it seems to me. May the Lord give us more time to prepare ourselves.

Moses desired to see God's face, and you will remember the response he received; "You will see only my back; you cannot see my face" (Exod 33:23). Moses was not yet ready, although so close! But then, on the last day, when God comes to wipe away your tears, what Moses never saw will be unveiled to you, and you will have all of eternity to look . . .

Indeed, may God himself give us more time to prepare!

To the Very Depths of Tenderness

Let us proceed still further in our meditation of what the prophet announced to us, "God will wipe away the tears from every face."

Among all the faces we have mentioned there is one on whom we should now settle our gaze a little more fixedly, a face down which the tears also ran but which no one took the trouble to wipe away. This face is that of Christ. He too wept, as the Gospels tell us. He shed tears that no one wiped away, no one! Those tears are still on his face!

On that last day we will all be assembled from the four corners of the earth to behold the mystery; we will see the Father wipe away the tears of his Son . . . ! The unfathomable mystery of tenderness!

Only silence can receive this mystery. Heaven and earth will be silent. The Holy Spirit will be silent. The Father will be silent as he wipes away the tears of his Son, and the Son will receive in silence this act of tenderness.

Holy Trinity, you are worthy . . .

Father,
your tenderness envelops me
causing my tears to flow . . .
blessed tears!
tears of tenderness.

You are worthy, because in these tears
you come so humbly
to blend your tenderness with mine
and so unite me with you
in the mystery of your love.

Father,
I can do no more now than be still
and rest in worship.

Then, on that day,
the creation, overflowing with such great mystery,
will burst out suddenly in eternal praise.
All the guests upon the holy mountain
united by the Spirit of holiness with earth and heaven,
and with voices rising from the dark abyss,[2]
will celebrate the song of the prophet:

"Behold our Lord!
Behold the God in whom we have hoped!
Let us rejoice and be glad!
It is he, our Lord, from whom salvation comes."

2. See Rev 5:13